PRAISE FOR
YOU CALL THIS DEMOCRACY?

"Reading Rusch's book is like taking a breath of fresh air and being injected with a vial of hope. A real democracy is within our reach!"

—MARIA CARDONA, CNN/CNN EN ESPAÑOL POLITICAL COMMENTATOR

"A desperately needed reality check, resource, and call to action for readers of all ages."

—MARTHA BROCKENBROUGH, AUTHOR OF *ALEXANDER HAMILTON: REVOLUTIONARY* AND *UNPRESIDENTED*

"This is a powerful book—literally. It's a clear and compelling user's guide to our democracy that gives readers the knowledge and tools to make a difference right now."

—STEVE SHEINKIN, AUTHOR OF AMERICAN HISTORY BOOKS FOR YOUNG ADULTS, INCLUDING *BOMB: THE RACE TO BUILD—AND STEAL—THE WORLD'S MOST DANGEROUS WEAPON*

"Elizabeth Rusch has written an important, revealing, and feisty book that shines a light on the many ways our governmental system actually undermines democracy. I hope readers are galvanized by her suggestions—and take action."

—CYNTHIA LEVINSON, COAUTHOR OF *FAULT LINES IN THE CONSTITUTION: THE FRAMERS, THEIR FIGHTS, AND THE FLAWS THAT AFFECT US TODAY*

"This is an important book for our times. Thoroughly researched and easy to read, *You Call This Democracy?* belongs in the hands of every voter and future voter. Our democracy depends on it."

—WINIFRED CONKLING, AUTHOR OF *VOTES FOR WOMEN! AMERICAN SUFFRAGISTS AND THE BATTLE FOR THE BALLOT*

YOU CALL THIS DEMOCRACY?

How to fix our government and deliver power to the people

ELIZABETH RUSCH

HOUGHTON MIFFLIN HARCOURT

BOSTON   NEW YORK

FOR ALL AMERICANS.
THE FUTURE IS IN OUR HANDS.

hmhbooks.com

The illustrations in this book were done digitally in Photoshop.
The text type was set in ITC Legacy Serif.
The display type was set in Avenir Next Condensed
and Garden Grown.
Book design by Ellen Duda

Library of Congress Cataloging-in-Publication Data is available.
ISBN 978-0-358-17692-3 (hbk)
ISBN 978-0-358-38742-8 (pbk)
ISBN 978-0-358-33069-1 (ebook)

Manufactured in China
SCP 10 9 8 7 6 5 4 3 2 1
4500786967

CONTENTS

INTRODUCTION
Do You Live in a Democracy?

Americans are taught that we live in a democracy. But is that really true?

More than two hundred years ago, a group of people met in Philadelphia, Pennsylvania, with an ambitious goal—to create a government more perfect than any other seen on Earth. "We the People . . . in Order to form a more perfect Union . . ." they wrote. The founders of the United States of America started us on a path to democracy, which comes from the Greek words for people, *demos,* and for rule, *kratos.* In a democracy, the people rule.

The United States is a representative democracy, where the people rule by regularly electing representatives who make the laws that govern us all. But how democratic is our government really? And how well is it working?

Americans enjoy great freedoms: freedom of the press, freedom of speech, freedom to gather with fellow citizens, freedom to practice the religion of our choosing, freedom to protest when the government does not work as we think it should. But people have begun to suspect that something is not quite right with our democracy. They may be right.

Public trust in government is dangerously low, according to surveys by the Pew Research Center. Only one in five Americans trusts the federal government to do what is right most of the time. This distrust crosses party lines, with only 28 percent of Republicans and 15 percent of Democrats reporting confidence. These misgivings span racial, gender, and ethnic groupings as well as generations.

When asked to compare our political system to those in similar countries, only about a quarter of Americans rate it "above average" and only 15 percent consider it the "best in the world."

Much of this dissatisfaction comes from our government's failure to address the challenges people face. Millions struggle to pay for the most expensive health care in the world. Many skip the medical care or prescriptions they desperately need. Forty percent of Americans live paycheck to paycheck, unable to cover an emergency expense of just $400. About 40 million Americans live in poverty—including 15 million children.

Wildfires rage. Droughts destroy farms. Cities and towns are inundated with floodwaters. Little is being done to stop global climate change even though a record number of Americans (80 percent) think something should be done about it. And these are just a few of the important issues our country struggles to address.

Many American citizens are tired of gridlock and the partisan divisions splitting our country. But maybe the problem is not *We the People*. Maybe the problem is that our democracy is not living up to its promise. When we don't feel heard or represented by our government, when the laws passed don't seem to help our country, we get angry at each other. But perhaps we need to direct some of that anger and energy toward the structures of our democracy. Perhaps our government is failing us because of fundamental flaws in the system.

A basic principle of a representative democracy is one person, one vote; each citizen has an equal say in electing representatives and thus influencing the laws of the land. No one's vote should mean more than anyone else's. No one should be able to buy power. The weight of your vote shouldn't depend on whether you are rich or poor, live in a particular state or an urban or rural area, or are a member of particular political party. You shouldn't need to be a certain race or gender or religion to have a say about how our country works. The vote of each citizen should be equal.

Just how far has our democracy veered from that ideal?

You've probably heard of the Electoral College, but you may not realize that this strange process actually takes a very important decision, who gets to be president, out of the hands of the people. You may know about some differences between the U.S. House of Representatives and the Senate, but you may not be aware that the Senate gives more power to people who live in smaller states. You may have heard of congressional districts, but you might be surprised to learn that when legislators redraw district borders, they can deliberately shift power to some voters and away from others.

This book examines issues such as these to explore several questions: How does our democracy live up to the principle of one person, one vote? Is political power equally accessible to all citizens? What would it take to build "a more perfect Union"?

This is not a civics textbook—though I hope readers will take away a deeper understanding of our government. It is not a political history of the United States—though some historical context will be given. It is also not a partisan plea designed to get readers to support one party or issue—though parties and issues may be mentioned in examples. Instead, this book tackles how our democracy really functions *today*, who really has power and why—and how that influences politicians and policies. It is my hope that this book unifies all people around the promise of democracy, that it gives an honest view of how our government really works, what is wrong, and what we can do together to fix it.

The hard truth—recognized by scholars, politicians, journalists, and public servants of all political persuasions—is that our system is rigged against ordinary Americans. We cannot fix the issues that matter to us until we fix the system. Whether you care about safe streets, a fair and effective justice system, immigration reform, the environment, the military, gay rights, the right to bear arms, or the right to prevent gun violence; whether you worry about wages, the cost of college, or our broken health care system; whether you are more concerned about clean air and water or the small-business tax burden, you need to pay attention to how decisions are made. For our democracy to work effectively on any issue, it must be responsive to the will of the people.

I admit, working on this book often made me angry—even outraged—when I saw clearly how some aspects of our democracy hurt fellow citizens. But my research has made me hopeful, too. Countless people, young and old, are already working to form a more perfect union.

Inspired by their work, this book is, ultimately, a book of solutions. After revealing flaws in our democracy, each chapter shows how we can address them and offers a bounty of organizations, websites, and other resources to get started.

Change is in our reach. Our country is ready for reform. Roughly two-thirds of Americans think "significant changes" need to be made to the "design and structure" of our government, according to a 2018 Pew poll. Citizen campaigns for reform in Michigan, Florida, North Dakota, and other places around the country have proven that the power of the people can beat the power of money, the power of habit, and the power of party politics.

As anthropologist Margaret Mead said, "Never doubt that a small group of thoughtful, committed citizens can change the world; indeed, it's the only thing that ever has."

Note: To the best of the author's knowledge, the information in this book was true when it went to press. Government and policy are rapidly evolving areas, though, and readers should follow the news and explore links in the book for the most current information. Updates will also be available at youcallthis.com.

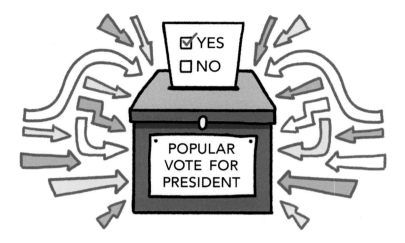

E very four years, voters across the country cast ballots to fill the highest government position in the country: president of the United States. They scan the list of candidates and mark a box by their choice, confident that they have had a say in this important decision.

But read the ballot's fine print, and you might find something like this: "A ballot cast for President and Vice President of the United States is considered a ballot cast for the slate of presidential electors nominated by the political party."

You don't vote for president. Someone else does it for you.

Though Americans vote on the first Tuesday in November, the president and vice president are not actually elected then.

Instead, every state is allocated a number of people called "electors" equal to the number of the state's U.S. senators and representatives. For example, New Jersey has two senators and twelve members in the House of Representatives, so the state has fourteen electors.

About a month after the election, the electors meet in their state capitals to cast their votes. Though the electors from all the states never gather in one place, they are traditionally called the Electoral College. Currently, the candidate who receives at least 270 out of 538 possible electoral votes wins the presidency.

This may be the oddest feature of our democracy—that we citizens don't get to elect our president (or vice president). It's also the most undemocratic.

> WE HAVE MORE THAN FIVE HUNDRED THOUSAND ELECTED OFFICIALS IN AMERICA. ALL WIN OFFICE BY WINNING THE MOST VOTES, EXCEPT TWO— THE PRESIDENT AND VICE PRESIDENT.

WHY ELECTORS?

This strange system is a relic from a very different time in U.S. history. In 1787, the new citizens of America had little experience electing national leaders. They were used to having a king. In the eighteenth century, when our founders gathered to create our system of government at the Constitutional Convention, they worried that tricky long-distance communication and transportation would make it difficult to properly inform voters about candidacies. They had no telephones, television, or even telegraphs; mail and newspapers were delivered by coach.

These days, we have plenty of experience directly voting for officials—and with television, computers, and the internet, people have access to loads of information about all the candidates and issues.

Another concern at the time was education. Founders thought it prudent to leave the decision to fewer, better-educated citizens. Today, with twelve years of free, public education available to everyone, literacy is near universal in the United States.

Some founders also wanted a backup plan to correct mistakes made by uneducated and unruly voters. Alexander Hamilton wrote that electors would stop someone with "talents for low intrigue and the little arts of popularity" from taking the top office and further prevent "foreign powers to an improper ascendant in our councils." In other words, Hamilton hoped electors would prevent a popular but corrupt candidate or someone strongly influenced by foreign powers from taking office.

But that is not how electors operate today. Electors are chosen by their political parties for their party loyalty, so they are not likely to vote for the other party's candidate. In addition, many state laws require electors to vote for the candidate that won that state's election. Electors have become no more than a rubber stamp for the statewide elections.

THE ELECTORAL

WA 12
MT 3
ND 3
MN 10
OR 7
ID 4
WY 3
SD 3
WI 10
MI 16
NV 6
UT 6
CO 9
NE 5
IA 6
IL 20
IN 11
OH 18
CA 55
AZ 11
NM 5
KS 6
MO 10
KY 8
WV 5
VA 13
AK 3
HI 4
OK 7
AR 6
TN - 11
NC 15
SC 9
TX 38
LA 8
MS 6
AL 9
GA 16
FL 29
VT 3
NH 4
ME 4
MA 11
NY 29
RI
CT 7
PA 20
NJ 14
DE 3
MD 10
DC 3

START

States get the same number of electors as they have members of Congress: the number of representatives + two senators

STATES APPOINT ELECTORS

FIRST TUESDAY IN NOVEMBER

Voters elect electors.

NOVEMBER

State election officials tally votes.

SHUFFLE!

FIRST MONDAY AFTER SECOND WEDNESDAY IN DECEMBER

Electors meet in state capitals across the country to vote.

DECEMBER

Each state sends the electors' votes to Congress.

JANUARY 6

President of U.S. Senate, in presence of all of Congress, opens the certificates, counts them, and declares the winner of the election.

JANUARY 20

President is inaugurated.

WINNERS LOSE

When this strange, outdated system works, the winner of the electoral vote and the nationwide popular vote—the actual tally of the citizen's votes—are the same. But sometimes the system fails, defying the will of the people, awarding the presidency to the loser of the popular vote and putting the election and the effectiveness of our democracy in doubt.

The problem lies in how elections are run at the state level. In forty-eight states and the District of Columbia, the presidential candidate who wins the statewide election gets *all* of that state's electoral votes. This is called "winner takes all." Compare that with a national popular vote, in which we would simply add together citizens' votes—just like we do for all other elections.

This "winner takes all" approach distorts reality. For example, if a state has ten electors, and a candidate wins 51 percent of the vote, that candidate gets all ten electoral votes. It's as if the candidate won 100 percent of the popular vote in that state, even though 49 percent voted for the opponent.

These state-by-state distortions can add up. Five times in our short history (1824, 1876, 1888, 2000, 2016), the candidate who won the highest number of citizens' votes did not take office. Because of our electoral system, the popular-vote winner lost.

This will likely keep happening. In 2016, a study by National Public Radio found that it's possible for a candidate to win the Electoral College with less than a quarter of the popular vote!

WINNERS WHO LOST

POPULAR VOTE WINNER

ELECTORAL VOTE WINNER

Hillary won the popular vote by 3 million votes

Hillary R. Clinton
65,844,063 votes

Donald J. Trump
62,980,062 votes

Donald J. Trump
304 votes

Hillary R. Clinton
227 votes

Albert Gore, Jr.
50,966,582 votes

George W. Bush
50,456,062 votes

George W. Bush
271 votes

Albert Gore, Jr.
266 votes

Grover Cleveland
5,540,309 votes

Benjamin Harrison
4,439,853 votes

Benjamin Harrison
233 votes

Grover Cleveland
168 votes

Samuel J. Tilden
4,300,590 votes

Rutherford B. Hayes
4,036,298 votes

Rutherford B. Hayes
185 votes

Samuel J. Tilden
184 votes

Can we really call ourselves a democracy if we hand the most powerful office to candidates who lose the popular vote?

FALLOUT: THE SUPREME COURT

It's easy to assume that because U.S. Supreme Court justices are appointed, not elected, the Electoral College has no impact on the court. Not so fast. Four of the nine currently serving U.S. Supreme Court justices were nominated by presidents who lost the popular vote. When presidents are elected by a minority of voters, chances are good the judges they appoint reflect minority opinions too. These appointments can have long-term impacts because Supreme Court justices do not have term limits. They serve for life.

CLOSE RACES AND TIES

In addition to being sorely out of date, the Electoral College system also leads to statewide recounts. A tight race in just one state can throw an entire presidential election into question. In 2000, the race in Florida came down to 537 votes. It took thirty-five days, with multiple attempts at recounting, and rulings from both the Florida State Supreme Court and U.S. Supreme Court, to settle the question of who would become president. The process left many questioning the outcome of the election.

There have been a few almost-misses too. In 2004, a shift of just sixty thousand votes to John Kerry (D) in Ohio would have cost George W. Bush (R) the election, despite Bush's 3-million-vote lead nationwide. In 1976, a shift of roughly nine thousand votes in Hawaii and Ohio would have wrested the presidency from Jimmy Carter (D), despite his almost 2-million-vote lead nationally over Gerald Ford (R).

The Constitution also dictates what happens if there is a tie in electoral votes or if no candidate wins a majority—and it's pretty undemocratic. The decision goes to the U.S. House of Representatives, where each state gets just one vote. That means Wyoming, representing about half a million people, gets the same say as Texas, with its close to *30 million* residents. It's hard to imagine a scenario farther from the principle of one person, one vote.

THE TIME ZONE PROBLEM

The founders did not know that our nation would grow to be massive, spanning several time zones. Our geography paired with the Electoral College discourages many citizens from voting. Imagine you are one of the 53 million people who live in the Pacific time zone—essentially California, Nevada, Oregon, and Washington. Your polling place is open until 8:00 p.m. and you plan to vote on your way home from work. But before arriving at the polls, you hear that one of the candidates has already won 270 electoral votes from statewide elections completed in earlier time zones. The contest has been decided. Why would you even bother to vote?

ONLY A FEW STATES MATTER

Perhaps the biggest problem with our electoral system starts long before any votes are cast. The Electoral College distorts campaigns by focusing the battle for the presidency on a few states rather than on the interests of the whole nation.

It is not the size of the state, the location of the state, or even the number of electoral votes that determines whether candidates care about your vote. It all depends on whether or not you live in a "battleground" or "swing" state, one with fairly equal numbers of Democratic and Republican voters. Candidates focus on winning those close races.

Citizens in the majority of states, the "spectator" states, have almost no say in picking the next leader of the country. When candidates already have a comfortable lead or sizable lag, they don't bother to meet with citizens in those states. They don't give speeches or attend rallies that might excite people about the issues. They don't poll or survey voters about their concerns. They don't pay for ads advocating for their positions or educating voters in those states. They don't even bother to try to register voters.

In 2012, for example, two-thirds of presidential campaign events happened in just four states: Ohio, Florida, Virginia, and Iowa. Thirty-eight states got *no* visits from candidates. These ignored states included almost all the rural, western, southern, and New England states. In 2016, two-thirds of the campaign events happened in just six states, with similar regions completely ignored.

BATTLEGROUND & SPECTATOR STATES

= Battleground States
= Spectator States

Source: Battleground states 2000-2020 according to 270 to Win

"If you're one of the four out of every five Americans who doesn't live in a battleground state, your voting doesn't count," says Saul Anuzis, former chair of Michigan's Republican Party, who supports a national popular vote. College sophomore Wynter Nelson knows firsthand what it's like to live in a spectator state. "It's kind of ridiculous because they push you and push you to vote, but then in the end, your vote doesn't really matter," she says. Maybe that is why voter turnout tends to be 11 percent lower in spectator states.

A RACIST HISTORY

When the Electoral College was created, enslaved people couldn't vote, so you might assume there was no connection between slavery and the Electoral College. You'd be wrong.

For the purposes of creating congressional districts *and* for handing out electors to states, the founders decided that black men would be counted as three-fifths of a person. Not only was this demeaning and dehumanizing, but it also ensured that southern states with large populations of enslaved people got more electors and thus had more say in electing the president even though blacks could not vote.

An international team of election experts who observed the 2016 U.S. elections saw the focus on battleground states and made a bold recommendation. They suggested that the United States reconsider the electoral system: "The aim of these proposals would be to ensure that presidential candidates campaign equally in all states and do not focus only on swing states," says the report from forty-one election experts and observers from eighteen countries. "In addition, they are an effort to ensure that public policy priorities are not distorted in an effort to win the vote of the most contested states."

Policy issues important to the few battleground states overshadow the interests of the country as a whole. As *Businessweek* noted: "[The] corn farmer living in Iowa is coveted by both parties and showered with goodies, such as ethanol subsidies. But just next door, the wheat grower in Republican South Dakota is insignificant to Presidential candidates. Ditto the hog farmer in Nebraska, the potato grower in Idaho, and the rancher in Oklahoma."

Money flows unevenly, too, with battleground states receiving about 7 percent more federal grant money than other states—and many more presidential disaster declarations. Andrew Reeves, a political scientist at Washington University, discovered that battleground states obtain double the number of disaster declarations as other states. Awarding disaster relief pays off in elections, he found. Each presidential declaration brought a 1 percent bump to that president's party come election time.

Does this seem fair? Do we want to keep having an election for the president of the Swing States of America, or is it time to try an election for the president of us all?

AMERICANS *WANT* TO ELECT THEIR PRESIDENT

Americans are ready to make the change. According to statewide and Gallup polls, roughly 70 percent of Americans favor switching to a nationwide popular vote, with little variation among Republicans, Democrats, and independents. That's almost three-quarters of Americans.

DIVIDED WE FALL

The Electoral College also shapes how we think of our democracy—in ways that are troubling. The typical Electoral College map is seared into the minds of many Americans. In it, states stand out boldly as deep blue (Democrat) along the West Coast and New England and stark red (Republican) in the South and Midwest. But this is a distortion of reality. Republicans and Democrats live all over our country. There is no such thing as a totally blue state or an all-red state—states are purple, made up of citizens who represent a mix of ideas, opinions, desires, and concerns.

The inaccurate oversimplification of the electoral map polarizes people. A Republican looking at the map might think, mistakenly, that she has no common ground with people in California. But more than 4 million Californians have supported Republicans in the last few elections. A Democrat might worry, mistakenly, that he would not be welcome in Alabama. But more than a third of Alabamans regularly vote Democratic.

A focus on the popular vote would remind us that people with all kinds of opinions live everywhere—it is the American way.

Tom Emmer (R), who ran for governor in Minnesota, thinks a national popular vote would encourage presidential candidates to run like governors do. "I had to run the entire state," he says. "I had to hit agricultural folks the same way I had to hit the folks on the Iron Range and it had to be consistent. [A popular vote] will transform national politics. You will see candidates run the entire country."

A presidential election based on a nationwide popular vote rather than state-by-state votes for electors would not only be fairer, it would also run more smoothly. A nationwide popular vote would create a massive pool of a couple of *hundred million* voters. This would likely create a much wider margin than in statewide races where margins can run in the hundreds, triggering recounts.

Finally, a popular vote would give every voter in the country a reason to participate. States might get serious about registering and encouraging voters as well. In the current system, it makes no difference if one person turns out to vote in a state or millions do; states are awarded the same number of electors. The national popular vote gives states an incentive to increase their power by energizing their citizens—and that is good for democracy.

So how can we make it happen?

THE STATE SOLUTION

The Electoral College was established through Article II, Section 1 of the U.S. Constitution. That means getting rid of the Electoral College would require a constitutional amendment. The U.S. House and Senate would have to pass the

WHAT IN THE WORLD?

Presidents all across the world—in Mexico, Ghana, Taiwan, and Argentina, for example—are elected by popular vote. In fact, we have the only presidential democracy on the planet with indirect elections through a mechanism like an electoral college instead of direct elections. "Electoral colleges are nowadays unknown, except for choosing politically weak ceremonial presidents," says Matthew Shugart, a professor of political science at the University of California, Davis, and coauthor of *A Different Democracy: A Systematic Comparison of the American System with Thirty Other Democracies.*

amendment by a two-thirds vote. Three-fourths (thirty-eight) of the fifty states would have to ratify, or formally agree to, the change. According to the National Archives, there have been more than seven hundred efforts to abolish or change the Electoral College by constitutional amendment. None have passed Congress. So that doesn't seem very promising.

There is another option.

In 2006, a computer scientist named John R. Koza proposed a different approach. When Koza was in his early twenties, he and some friends invented a board game based on the Electoral College. Later, Koza served as an elector in two presidential elections, but the role did not sit well with him. "The current system is insane and unjustifiable," he says. "It leaves at least 40 states out of the process."

He thought the popular vote was the right way to go and wondered how it could be accomplished. Then he learned about interstate compacts—where two or more states agree to handle something the same way. He realized that the Constitution itself holds the key to fixing the problem. The Constitution reads: "Each State shall appoint, in such Manner as the Legislature thereof may direct, a Number of Electors . . ." That opens the door for states to agree together to designate all their electors to whomever wins the nationwide popular vote!

In a press conference in 2006, Koza, along with Democratic, Republican, and independent members of Congress, introduced the National Popular Vote interstate compact. Within days the *Chicago Sun Times, New York Times,* and *Minneapolis Star-Tribune* endorsed the idea. "We say the United States is ready for real democracy," said the *Los Angeles Times.* "A system that produces a majority winner will boost political engagement across all 50 states," noted the *Denver Post.*

About a year later, Maryland became the first state to enact the compact. Soon, state legislators all across the country took up the bill. New Jersey signed it into law. Illinois became the third state, then Hawaii. The list is now fifteen states long (plus D.C.), representing 196 electoral votes.

MORE THAN THREE THOUSAND STATE LEGISLATORS HAVE SPONSORED OR VOTED FOR A NATIONAL POPULAR VOTE! HAVE YOURS?

The compact will take effect once states representing a total of 270 electoral votes—the number needed to win the presidency—have signed on. The endeavor is two-thirds of the way there, with just seventy-four more electoral votes needed. Efforts are afoot in a dozen or so states, which could get the tally to the magic 270.

If that happens, whether your vote matters won't depend on whether you live in a battleground or spectator state, in a heavily Republican or heavily Democratic state. Your vote—every vote—will count equally toward electing the president of the United States.

About a third of Americans say they want to keep the Electoral College as it is. They worry that any change would

THE NATIONAL POPULAR VOTE COMPACT

The 888-word bill already enacted by fifteen states reads:

"The State of _____ seeks to join with other states and establish the Agreement Among the States to Elect the President by National Popular Vote."

The bill provides that:

★ Each state will conduct an election for president and vice president.

★ Each state will allocate its electors to the "national popular vote winner."

★ In the event of a tie in the popular vote, states will award their electors to the winner of their state.

★ States can withdraw at any time except for the period six months before the end of a president's term until the successor has been chosen. (In other words, states cannot withdraw in the middle of a presidential election.)

be unconstitutional. But the Constitution gives states complete control to decide how to allocate electors. They worry that counting a national vote would be expensive. But it is not difficult to add up votes from fifty states and the District of Columbia; it already happens. They worry that small states will be ignored. But small spectator states are already ignored. They worry that the national popular vote will favor one party over another. But that will happen only if the American people favor one party over another, *which is how democracy is supposed to work.*

That's why the National Popular Vote has broad support in the Republican and Democratic parties. During debate over the measure in the Colorado Senate, Ken Gordon (D) said: "We think the president should be the person who gets the majority vote. It's the bedrock of our democracy." Kirk Dillard (R), Illinois state senator and chair of his local Republican party, felt the same. "This isn't a Democratic or Republican issue to me," he said. "It's important that people have faith that, in the election of the most important office in the world, their vote will count."

Organizations as diverse as the American Civil Liberties Union and the Conservative Party of New York endorse the National Popular Vote. Even electors recognize the folly of the process they participate in. Wisconsin electors adopted a resolution calling for the abolition of the Electoral College system.

A growing number of Americans agree that for a position as important to our country as the president of the United States, *every* vote in *every* state should count *equally* in *every* presidential election.

ROAD TO THE POPULAR VOTE

Check out this map.
Has your state signed on for the popular vote?

 National Popular Vote bill has been enacted

 State legislature has taken some action on the bill

◯ No state level action

Source: National Popular Vote

WHAT YOU CAN DO

The path to a national popular vote lies with states. The good news is that state legislators pay attention to phone calls, letters, emails, petitions, and visits from their constituents. And they welcome hearing from future voters in their district as well. Here's how to spread the word:

★ Find out if your state has enacted the National Popular Vote compact: www.nationalpopularvote.com/state-status.

★ If your state has not passed it yet, write, call, or email your governor and state representative and senator. Even better, set up a meeting. (You'll learn more about how to do this in chapter 12.) To identify your representatives, type in your zip code to Who Represents Me? to get their contact information: www.270towin.com/elected-officials.

★ Create a petition and gather signatures online here: www.change.org/start-a-petition.

★ Write letters to the editors of your local and statewide newspapers. (For your newspaper's address and submission process, search the internet for "Letters to the Editor" and the name of your newspaper.)

I do not recommend a Constitutional amendment lightly.
I think the amendment process must be reserved for an
issue of overriding governmental significance. But the
method by which we elect our President is such an issue.

—JIMMY CARTER (D), THIRTY-NINTH U.S. PRESIDENT

[P]riority must be accorded to electoral college reform.

—RICHARD NIXON (R), THIRTY-SEVENTH U.S. PRESIDENT

A national popular vote means that every vote in every city,
village, and town, in every state will count. And will count
equally. A vote in Buffalo will be the same as a vote in Boca
Raton. A vote in Corning will be as sought after as a vote in
Cleveland. Manhattan will matter as much as Miami.

—JEFFREY DINOWITZ (D), NEW YORK ASSEMBLY

Presidential elections should be a time when the entire
nation is galvanized into action through a vibrant democracy because every citizen has a voice in setting the
nation's direction for the next four years.

—JOSEPH GRIFFO (R), NEW YORK STATE SENATOR

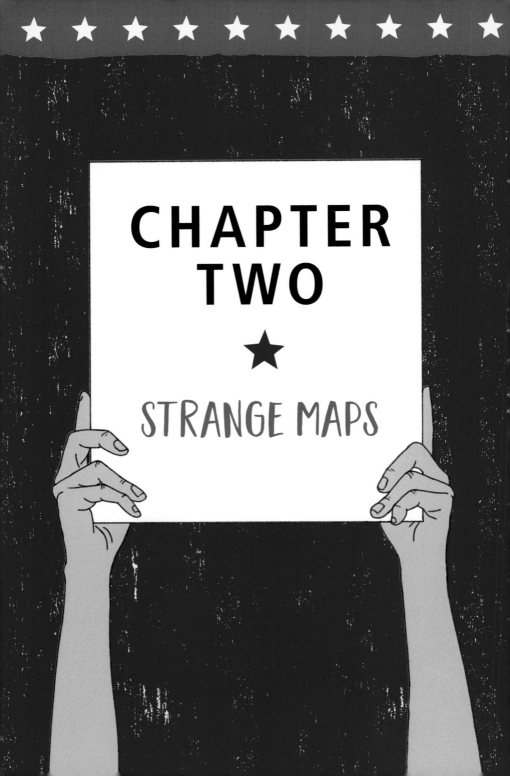

CHAPTER TWO

★

STRANGE MAPS

Twenty-six-year-old Katie Fahey was dreading Thanksgiving. She knew her family members had supported opposing candidates and parties in the 2016 election and that arguments would break out. "I didn't want another holiday to be ruined by divisiveness," she says. But she thought there was something they could all agree on. "Nobody trusted the system—on the right, on the left, in the middle," she says. So she decided to bring up an issue she hoped her whole family could get behind: ending gerrymandering.

IN A TRUE DEMOCRACY, VOTERS CHOOSE REPRESENTATIVES. GERRYMANDERING TURNS THIS PRINCIPLE ON ITS HEAD.

WHAT IS GERRYMANDERING?

In a true representative democracy, voters choose representatives. Gerrymandering turns this principle on its head—politicians draw weird borders for voting districts, essentially cherry-picking which voters will be in their districts.

The term *gerrymandering* was coined in 1812 when Massachusetts governor Elbridge Gerry approved a voting map for the state favoring his party. The map included a district that resembled a salamander, thus creating a "Gerry-mander." The *Salem Gazette* published a political cartoon and wrote that "this [map] inflicted a grievous wound on the Constitution."

Today's gerrymandered voting districts are equally outrageous. Many resemble blood spatters, horseshoes, cartoon characters, and bizarre tentacled monsters. The maps would be funny if they weren't so damaging to our democracy.

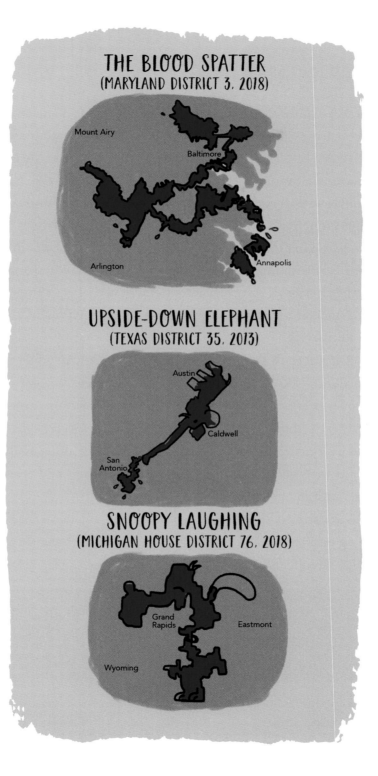

HOW REDISTRICTING IS SUPPOSED TO WORK

The U.S. House of Representatives is made up of 435 members representing 435 districts in the fifty states. (That number has been fixed by federal law since 1913.) Every ten years, the U.S. government conducts a census, counting everyone in the country. By law, each voting district must hold an equal number of people, roughly 711,000 at present. Within a year or two of the census, taking into account population changes, states draw new maps with new district borders. States also redraw maps for the election of state legislators. Redistricting is an important democratic practice, one that aims for equal representation for all citizens.

A number of common-sense principles should guide the drawing of voting district maps. One principle is compactness. Districts should keep voters from the same communities together, so they can advocate for their shared concerns about schools, traffic, access to health care, jobs, and other issues. This is especially important to ensure that racial and ethnic communities have a fair say.

The districts should also be contiguous, which means the voting district is one connected area. District lines should follow geographic features, keeping voters on the same side of a

REDISTRICTING IS AN IMPORTANT DEMOCRATIC PRACTICE, ONE THAT AIMS FOR EQUAL REPRESENTATION FOR ALL CITIZENS.

river or mountain together; keeping members of the same city, town, or county together, and keeping the same school districts and other local government areas together.

Likewise, districts should preserve communities of interest. It makes sense, if possible, to give urban, suburban, and rural areas their own districts so their views are represented. Similarly, a community that borders a wildfire-prone area or a river that floods frequently might want to be able to speak with one voice to candidates.

HOW TO DRAW AN UNFAIR MAP

Katie Fahey discovered that, to her dismay, the people drawing voting maps often have a stake in how they're drawn. In the 2018 election, in thirty-four states, including her own state of Michigan, *state legislators* had drawn their own district maps. That allowed politicians from the party in power to tinker with the boundaries of voting districts to give an advantage to their party and ensure that they and their friends would stay in office.

Instead of drawing simple shapes or following natural features like river or neighborhood borders, politicians often draw district lines to contain voters they think will reelect them. They draw maps to protect people already in office (called incumbents), to undermine political foes, and to fracture communities that might vote together to remove them from office. "A lot of people don't think about gerrymandering because they don't realize it is a manipulated system," says Fahey.

"When you're heading to work, making sure your kids get to day care, you're not stopping to think: 'Oh, I wonder how my voting district is drawn.'"

UNFAIR VERSUS FAIR MAPS

Compare these two voting district maps for the same part of Pennsylvania. The gerrymandered map on the left shows horseshoe-shaped District 7, which was used from 2012 to 2018. The map on the right shows the same area after the Pennsylvania Supreme Court threw out the gerrymandered map and redrew a new one in 2018. The new district (right) includes all of Delaware County and keeps a chunk of Philadelphia suburbs in one district.

Mucking with voting maps can determine the outcomes of elections before anyone votes, preordaining who represents us in the U.S. House of Representatives, in state legislatures, and even on local councils or school boards. The magazine *Mother Jones* describes how Democrats tinkered with a district in Maryland to gain a U.S. House seat: "Democrats added a strange-looking appendage to the district, reaching all the way down into the affluent Washington, D.C., suburbs to scoop up

Democratic voters. More than 360,000 people were moved out of the district, and nearly as many were moved in. It went from solidly Republican to reliably Democratic."

Gerrymandering is not a healthy practice. "Partisan gerrymandering leads to dysfunction, polarization, and the legitimate belief held by average Americans that, for them, our political system just does not work," says former attorney general Eric Holder. "Regardless of party affiliation, that's not good for our democracy."

GERRYMANDERING: THE GAME

Gerrymandering seemed so bizarre to seventeen-year-old Josh Lafair that he and his brothers created a board game called *Mapmaker: The Gerrymandering Game*. "It has all the right mechanics of a board game—scheming, strategizing, backstabbing," said Lafair. Their marketing materials for the game proclaim: "Can you create unfair, lopsided, strangely shaped districts that will guarantee your party's victory? Gerrymandering with friends and family (when it doesn't affect real voters) is a whole lot of fun." Lafair knows that gerrymandering in practice is bad for our country. He wants his game to raise awareness of the antidemocratic custom and has raised money to send the game to legislators across the country and to all the U.S. Supreme Court judges.

How are maps manipulated? To gain an unfair advantage, the party in power might "crack" (or split into multiple districts) voters from the opposing party so they can't reach a majority. For example, for years, many of the ten thousand students of North Carolina A&T University supported an African American Democrat. "This many students has the ability to sway any election," says Love Caesar, a sophomore at the historically black college. But after the 2010 census, the North Carolina state legislature drew a new voting map. They removed the campus from the 12th District and cut the campus in half, placing students into Districts 6 and 13, which were predominantly white. "I think that people in the state legislature are smart, and I think they knew what they were doing," says senior Braxton Brewington. "To have six dorms on one side and six dorms on the other is just too coincidental." The resulting District 12 went from black majority to black minority. With their votes split, the students no longer had a sufficient majority in either district to sway the election toward their preferred candidates. Instead, with the new district boundaries, students were represented by two conservative white Republicans.

GERRYMANDERING HAS BEEN USED TO UNDERMINE THE VOTING POWER OF PEOPLE OF COLOR.

Another technique is to "pack" voters from the opposing party into as few districts as possible. That way the opposing party will overwhelmingly win those seats but have no power anywhere else in the state. When Eric Mansfield (D), an African

American doctor, first ran for the North Carolina state Senate in 2010, his northwest Fayetteville district was racially and economically diverse, with black and white voters, rich and poor voters. Mansfield reached out to them all. In a district with 45 percent black voters, he won the election with 67 percent of the vote.

When Republicans redrew the voting maps, they surgically added long tentacles to Mansfield's district reaching into black neighborhoods. The new map, which resembled an octopus, packed black people into his district until they made up 51 percent of his constituents. "I didn't need the help," says Mansfield, whose own street was split into two districts. He was also upset that he no longer represented most of the people in his predominantly white neighborhood, many of whom had been his patients.

BAD FOR PEOPLE OF COLOR, BAD FOR US ALL

You might notice a racial component to these two examples. Gerrymandering has been used to undermine the voting power of people of color. Historically, racial gerrymanders spread minority voters among districts, like in the university example, so they didn't have enough voting power in any one district to elect someone who understood their experiences and interests.

For a while, the Voting Rights Act of 1965 prohibited splitting, or cracking, the votes this way. Instead, states concentrated, or packed, the minority vote into few districts.

CAN YOU GERRYMANDER?

See for yourself how representation can depend on how you draw the map. This "state" has 50 people. The majority, 60 percent, support dark blue candidates. Forty percent support the other party. How many ways could you group these voters into five equal districts, ten people per district?

How do you draw the map so the five districts are proportional, with three dark blue districts and two light blue?

Can you draw the map so that dark blue wins ALL five races?

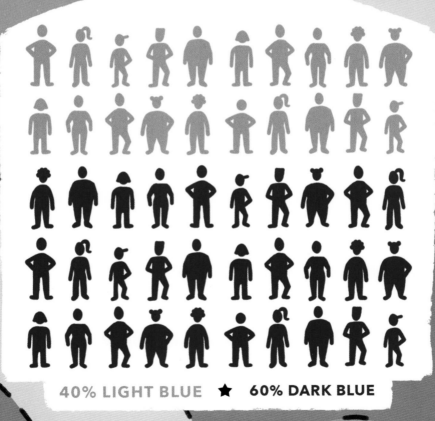

40% LIGHT BLUE ★ 60% DARK BLUE

Light blue is in the minority with only forty percent of the vote. Can you draw the district lines so that they win the majority (three out of five) of the seats?

HERE'S ONE WAY:

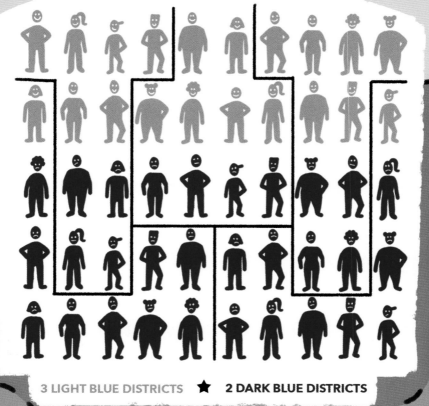

3 LIGHT BLUE DISTRICTS ★ 2 DARK BLUE DISTRICTS

But this hurt people of color too. "If you have too high a percent African Americans in a House district," says David Canon, professor of political science at the University of Wisconsin–Madison, "it does dilute the overall representation of African American interests."

But gerrymandering affects people of all backgrounds. Drawing districts where everyone knows who is going to win and who is going to lose means that candidates don't have to fight for your vote. They don't have to listen to voters or try to win people over by supporting popular policies.

Worst of all, gerrymandering, rather than the popular vote, can decide elections. In 2012, a majority of North Carolinians cast their votes for Democrats. Based on the results of the popular vote, you'd expect Democrats to have won seven seats in the U.S. House of Representatives, and Republicans to have taken six. But the gerrymandered map packed almost all of the Democratic voters into a few districts. So four Democrats and nine Republicans went to Washington. Likewise, in Pennsylvania, a state that has roughly equal numbers of Democrats and Republicans, a gerrymandered map helped send *five* Democrats and *thirteen* Republicans to Congress. When the Pennsylvania Supreme Court threw out the map and drew a new one in 2018, representation evened out, with nine representatives from each party going to Washington.

GERRYMANDERING, RATHER THAN OUR VOTES, CAN DECIDE ELECTIONS.

When one party dominates state legislatures and governorships across the country—currently Republicans—all those state gerrymanders can add up to a Congress that does not represent the people. In 2012, Democratic House candidates earned about 1.2 million more votes than Republican candidates. So they should have won the majority of House seats. Instead, Republicans won thirty-three more seats.

Research suggests that gerrymandering is getting worse. Nicholas Stephanopoulos of the University of Chicago Law School reviewed voting districts from 1972 to 2012. He found

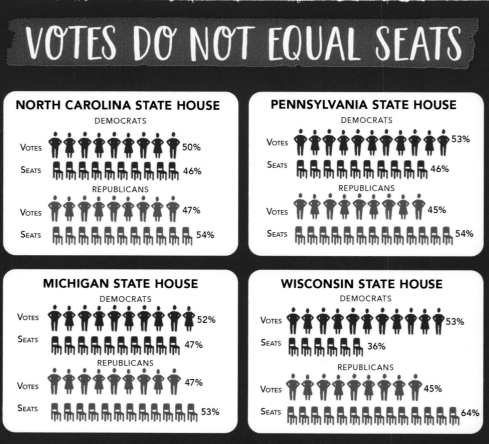

VOTES DO NOT EQUAL SEATS

NORTH CAROLINA STATE HOUSE

DEMOCRATS
VOTES 50%
SEATS 46%

REPUBLICANS
VOTES 47%
SEATS 54%

PENNSYLVANIA STATE HOUSE

DEMOCRATS
VOTES 53%
SEATS 46%

REPUBLICANS
VOTES 45%
SEATS 54%

MICHIGAN STATE HOUSE

DEMOCRATS
VOTES 52%
SEATS 47%

REPUBLICANS
VOTES 47%
SEATS 53%

WISCONSIN STATE HOUSE

DEMOCRATS
VOTES 53%
SEATS 36%

REPUBLICANS
VOTES 45%
SEATS 64%

Source: MSNBC.com and Ballotpedia.org

that "over this period as a whole, the typical plan was fairly balanced and neither party enjoyed a systemic advantage" while "plans in effect [in 2012 were] the most extreme gerrymanders in modern history."

Technology is one reason for the shift. Parties in power often hire consultants to mine voting and demographic data and use computer programs to draw the most advantageous maps. "It's easier than ever to create skewed maps," says Michael Li, a redistricting expert with the Brennan Center for Justice at the New York University School of Law. "There's much more robust data and sophisticated technology than there used to be. Gerrymandering was once an art. Now it's a science."

WHAT IN THE WORLD?

Not many other democracies in the world let politicians draw their own voting districts, according to a study by Lisa Handley of Frontier International Electoral Consulting. Canada did for many years and had a nasty gerrymandering problem to show for it. But in the 1960s, the country shifted to having three-person independent commissions draw the maps for each province. "Today, most [districts] are simple and uncontroversial, chunky and geometric, and usually conform to the vague borders of some geographic/civic region knowable to the average citizen who lives there," wrote J. J. McCullough, a political commentator in Vancouver, British Columbia.

BOTH PARTIES GERRYMANDER

It's a science used by Democrats and Republicans alike. A 2012 analysis by the Brennan Center showed that in the states where Republicans drew the congressional maps, their candidates won 53 percent of the popular vote but took 72 percent of the seats. Likewise, where Democrats drew the maps, their candidates won 56 percent of the vote but took over 71 percent of the seats.

Legislators are surprisingly up front about what they're doing. In 2011, for example, Wisconsin state senator Dale Schultz (R) was invited to review a draft of the voting map his party had drawn. "I took one look at the map and saw that if I chose to run for reelection I could win, no trouble," he recalls. And he was right—he won easily. "I'd never seen anything like that before. I started to see how powerful and unbelievable the redistricting process was."

Members of both parties speak openly about their partisan gerrymandering. A Democratic governor said: "Part of my intent was to create a map that, all things being legal and equal, would, nonetheless, be more likely to elect more Democrats rather than less." A Republican state legislator told his colleagues: "I think electing Republicans is better than electing Democrats. So I drew this map to help foster what I think is better for the country."

Parties in the minority in their state government have tried to fight gerrymandering. State senator Jeff Jackson (D) of Charlotte, North Carolina, saw this firsthand. When Republicans wanted to end gerrymandering, "My side always took those bills they filed and threw them in the trash can because we never thought we'd be out of power," he recalls. "Then as soon as it switched and the Democrats were in the minority, the first thing we said was, 'Hey, how about independent redistricting?' And the first thing Republicans said was, 'How about epic payback?'"

But *voters* in both parties want to end gerrymandering. In 2013, a Harris Poll found that three-quarters of Republicans said that politicians who stand to benefit from redistricting should not control the mapmaking. Similar percentages of Democrats and independents agreed. "People instinctively get this," says Michael Li of the Brennan Center for Justice.

IS IT CONSTITUTIONAL?

Gerrymandering may violate our First Amendment freedom of speech. Maps based on past voting records and party affiliation punishes some people for their political speech. "What's really shocking is that in front of our eyes for years, the states have been moving people from one [district] to another based on the views they have expressed . . . because you have identified yourself as Democrat or Republican," says Thomas Geoghegan of the nonpartisan League of Women Voters.

Gerrymandering may also violate the Fourteenth Amendment, which requires "equal protection of the law."

"When you're talking about the opportunity to turn your vote into a policy change, the Fourteenth Amendment says you should have an equal chance, whether you're a Democrat or a Republican," according to Ruth Greenwood of the Campaign Legal Center. That is not true when maps are gerrymandered.

For a while, state supreme courts ruled in defense of voters' rights. In 2018, Pennsylvania judges threw out the state's map and drew a new one. Judges in North Carolina have thrown out maps three times. But then the U.S. Supreme Court weighed in. In June 2019, it overturned lower court decisions in North Carolina and Maryland. In the 5 to 4 decision, Chief Justice John Roberts wrote that while "excessive partisanship in districting leads to results that reasonably seem unjust," fixing the problem is "beyond the reach of federal courts." The ruling rendered courts powerless to address partisan gerrymandering.

The result: The gerrymandered maps in North Carolina and Maryland will remain in place. Court challenges to gerrymandered maps in other states, such as Ohio and Michigan, will also likely fail. Republicans can keep drawing maps to elect the most Republicans, Democrats can keep drawing maps to elect the most Democrats—and lawsuits won't work. The courts' hands have been tied.

In a scathing dissent to the ruling, Justice Elena Kagan called partisan gerrymandering "anti-democratic in the most profound sense" and said the practice "debased and dishonored our democracy, turning upside-down the core American idea that all governmental power derives from the people."

In the wake of the Supreme Court ruling, gerrymandering could get worse. "Expect the abuse to be supercharged," said Justin Levitt, associate dean of Loyola Law School. "Now the answer will be, 'It happens everywhere.' Expect the [gerrymandering] disease to spread."

Unless citizens do something about it…

POWER TO THE CITIZENS

Katie Fahey of Michigan figured citizens needed to step in to make this right. "A lot of people understand that politicians [will be] politicians," Fahey says, "and that them being able to control the outcome of elections doesn't makes sense." So she posted on Facebook: "I'd like to take on gerrymandering in Michigan. If you're interested in doing this as well please let me know." *Thousands* of people responded.

Fahey had never been part of a political campaign before. She and the other volunteers decided to hold thirty-three town meetings to gather ideas from fellow citizens on how to create a fair redistricting system.

RESEARCH SUGGESTS THAT FAIR MAPS ARE MORE LIKELY TO BE DRAWN IF WE TAKE CONTROL OUT OF THE HANDS OF POLITICIANS AND PUT IT INTO THE HANDS OF CITIZENS.

Fahey's citizen group, called Voters Not Politicians, decided to turn over mapmaking in Michigan to a thirteen-member independent citizens' commission made up of four members of the majority party, four members of the minority party, and five third-party or independent voters.

This approach is backed by research, which suggests that fair maps are more likely to be drawn if we take control out of the hands of politicians and put it into the hands of citizens. A study of voting maps conducted by the Brennan Center for

Justice found that maps drawn by independent commissions exhibit much lower levels of partisan bias. Alaska, Arizona, California, Idaho, Iowa, Montana, and Washington already use independent commissions to draw voting maps, and gerrymandering is virtually nonexistent in those states.

Fahey's group began collecting signatures to put their plan, Proposal 2, on the 2018 statewide ballot, with her family joining the effort. Volunteers brought their clipboards to parades, festivals, and football games. They gathered almost half a million signatures—more than enough to get Proposal 2 on the ballot. Fahey's mother, who didn't even know what gerrymandering was at first, collected seven hundred signatures.

CITIZEN SUCCESS

Ordinary citizens have had enormous success outlawing gerrymandering. In 2008, California's Proposition 11 turned state redistricting over to a nonpartisan citizen's commission. In May 2018, voters in Ohio passed a ballot measure requiring bipartisan cooperation in drawing congressional districts.

Li of the Brennan Center called the 2018 midterm result "a huge win for the reformers." Missouri citizens voted to create a nonpartisan mapmaking position and institute strict redistricting criteria. Voters in Colorado and Utah passed ballot measures to end gerrymandering by establishing independent commissions.

In Michigan, Li was surprised that Katie Fahey's group of unpaid volunteers could even gather enough signatures to get on the ballot. Fahey herself expected her effort to fail: "It actually takes usually more than one try," she says.

ORDINARY CITIZENS HAVE HAD ENORMOUS SUCCESS OUTLAWING GERRYMANDERING.

But Michigan Proposal 2, the Independent Redistricting Commission Initiative, passed—with more than 60 percent of the vote. Fahey couldn't be prouder. "It was a lot of work," she says. "But thousands of people showed that regular people can amend the [state] Constitution when we need to, when there is a problem."

Citizens continue to be on the move to stop gerrymandering before the next census. Volunteers in Arkansas are working to get a seven-member citizen redistricting commission on the 2020 ballot. A group called Represent Oklahoma is working to change the state constitution to end gerrymandering by 2021. And citizens are putting pressure on state legislatures in Virginia and Pennsylvania to end gerrymandering.

Pennsylvanian Rose Reeder started with one phone call—to her board of county commissioners. She prepared posters on gerrymandering and presented them to the commission.

"REGULAR PEOPLE CAN AMEND THE CONSTITUTION WHEN WE NEED TO, WHEN THERE IS A PROBLEM."

The commissioners voted unanimously to endorse an independent commission to draw district lines. So Reeder visited all thirty counties. "I'd go in, and they were looking tired and thinking, 'I hope she hurries up,'" Reeder recalls. "As I presented, I could see them sitting a little straighter, more attentive. I could see that they changed their attitude." All thirty commissions passed resolutions asking the state legislature to end gerrymandering.

It's citizen work that makes all the difference, says Fahey. Passing the measure to end gerrymandering in her state was "a strong move toward restoring some faith in our democracy," she says. "The really cool part is it was only possible because of the thousands of people who stepped up to make it happen."

WHAT YOU CAN DO

Start Now!

The federal government is conducting a census in 2020. Based on the results, states will redraw district lines in 2021 and 2022. So the time to outlaw gerrymandering is *now*.

Encourage Congress

Advancing reform through federal law is possible but not promising. In 2005, 2007, and 2009, U.S. Rep. John Tanner (D) of Tennessee introduced a bill requiring states to appoint independent bipartisan redistricting commissions and establishing national districting guidelines. But neither national party has taken the bill seriously. After Tanner retired, Rep. Jim Cooper (D) took up the banner, introducing the John Tanner Fairness and Independence in Redistricting Act into Congress. Check to see if your members of Congress have signed on as cosponsors and encourage them to do so here: www.congress .gov/bill/115th-congress/house-bill/712/cosponsors.

Learn about other congressional bills on redistricting at www.brennancenter.org/analysis/redistricting-reform-tracker -congressional-bills.

Fix Your State

As Fahey and others have shown, we can fix gerrymandering without going to Congress or the courts. Lobby your state legislature to require redistricting by an independent citizen's commission. Find out what is happening in your state at www .brennancenter.org/issues/redistricting.

You can also learn about and get involved in state redistricting campaigns through Common Cause: www.commoncause .org/state-redistricting-campaigns/#.

Sign up for events such as making phone calls or texting voters who support fair districting at events.mobilizeamerica .io/ndrc.

You may also be able to go around politicians and straight to other citizens by placing a referendum on a statewide ballot.

Twenty-six states allow ballot initiatives. Find out what is possible in your state here: ballotpedia.org/States_with_initiative _or_referendum.

Be Nonpartisan

No matter your approach, make it clear that your efforts are all about creating fair elections rather than putting a particular party in power. Try to build support for reform in both parties and from nonpartisan groups such as the League of Women Voters and the Rotary Club. For example, in Ohio, reformers got endorsements from every living former governor of the state, Republican and Democrat.

Show the Weirdness

Never underestimate the power of public opinion. Everything you do to rally support to end gerrymandering has the potential to pressure legislators into doing the right thing. One way to draw attention to this problem is to show how strange the voting lines are by traveling their edges. In September 2014, a group of citizens in Maryland walked, ran, cycled, and boated the 225 miles across Maryland's District 3 to demonstrate that voting districts are not supposed to be, as one judge put it, "reminiscent of a broken-winged pterodactyl, lying prostrate across the center of the state." Plan a bike trip, relay race, or treasure hunt through a gerrymandered district and invite the public and the media, and post on social media. Make sure to propose a better map or method.

Draw Your Own Map!

The artists out there can make fun of the strange shapes created by gerrymandered maps and sketch out more common-sense alternatives to share with the media and legislators. Virginia, New York, and Massachusetts have all held competitions for citizens to draw voting district maps. You can, too. Send your maps to the media, your state representatives, and senators, and post them on social media.

Include Communities of Color

Because gerrymandering has been used to weaken the political power of communities of color, it's essential that these citizens not be further harmed by reform. Make sure proposals reflect their views and needs and prioritize fair representation of their communities.

It's time to terminate gerrymandering.

ARNOLD SCHWARZENEGGER (R), FORMER GOVERNOR OF CALIFORNIA

Partisan gerrymanders are incompatible with democratic principles.

—SUPREME COURT JUSTICE RUTH BADER GINSBURG, APPOINTED BY PRESIDENT BILL CLINTON (D)

[Gerrymandering] is cancerous, undermining the fundamental tenets of our form of democracy.

—FEDERAL JUDGE PAUL NIEMEYER, APPOINTED BY PRESIDENT GEORGE H.W. BUSH (R)

Americans deserve better. Congressional representation should not be a political blood sport that protects incumbents, disenfranchises legitimate interests, and allows people to achieve with surgical reappointment what they couldn't do honestly at the ballot box.

—OREGON MEMBER OF CONGRESS EARL BLUMENAUER (D)

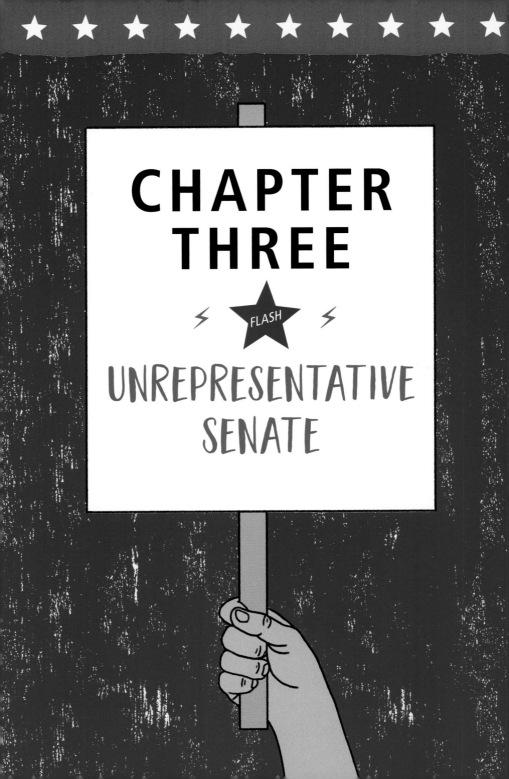

While gerrymandering can determine seats in the U.S. House of Representatives, it can't touch the U.S. Senate. That's because Senate seats are won in statewide elections. That's the good news.

The bad news is that the Senate itself undermines the principle of one person, one vote. "The gravest threat to fair representation is the mandate that each state elects two senators to the U.S. Senate regardless of population, a system that has created perhaps the most unrepresentative legislative chamber in the world," says Daniel Wirls, a professor of politics at the University of California, Santa Cruz, and coauthor of the book *The Invention of the United States Senate.*

The problem is that giving each state equal representation takes power from voters in states with large populations and gives it to voters from small states. Vermont's 624,000 citizens are represented by two senators and so are New York's *20 million.* That gives a voter from Vermont more than thirty times the power of a New York voter. Compare Wyoming's 574,000 people with California's *40 million* people and the distortion of voting power is even worse.

"By 2040, 70 percent of Americans are expected to live in the 15 largest states, which are also home to the overwhelming majority of the 30 largest cities in the country," says David Birdsell, a political science professor at Baruch College. "That means that 70 percent of Americans get all of 30 Senators and 30 percent of Americans get 70 Senators."

The problem affects both Democrats and Republicans, who each hold majorities in large states. For example, the 29 million residents of Republican-leaning Texas receive the same number of senators as the 1 million residents of Democratic-leaning Rhode Island. "It's a grotesque misrepresentation," Professor Wirls says.

The composition of the Senate was a compromise our founders made in 1787 to get small states to sign the Constitution. But many founders, including Alexander Hamilton, recognized and despised how undemocratic the Senate would be. As Hamilton wrote in Federalist paper No. 22, "Every idea of proportion and every rule of fair representation conspire to condemn a principle, which gives to Rhode Island an equal

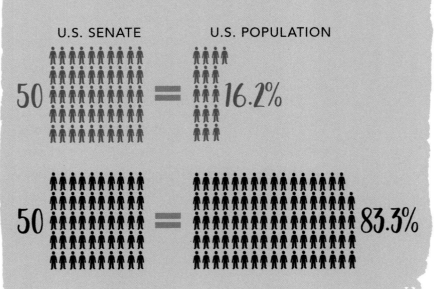

HALF OF SENATORS REPRESENT
JUST *16 PERCENT* OF THE U.S. POPULATION

U.S. SENATE   U.S. POPULATION

50 = 16.2%

50 = 83.3%

weight in the scale of power with Massachusetts, or Connecticut, or New York; and to Delaware an equal voice in the national deliberations with Pennsylvania, or Virginia, or North Carolina. Its operation contradicts the fundamental maxim of republican government, which requires that the sense of the majority should prevail."

Nowadays, small states, even though they represent less than 20 percent of the U.S. population, can theoretically elect a Senate majority, according to Frances Lee, professor of government and politics at the University of Maryland.

People living in large states are denied laws they support and a fair share of government funding. Research suggests federal funding flows disproportionately to small states. "From highway bills to homeland security, small states make out like bandits," says Sarah Binder, a political scientist at George Washington University. People of color, who tend to live in larger states, suffer disproportionately from this underrepresentation.

The unrepresentative Senate can even affect court rulings. Because of the makeup of the Senate, a U.S. Supreme Court judge can be confirmed with support from senators who represent a very narrow portion of America's views and values. The most recent example is Brett Kavanaugh, who was confirmed to the U.S. Supreme Court with votes from senators representing only 44 percent of the population.

It's bad enough that the Senate undermines the fair and equal representation of all citizens. But the Senate follows some odd rules that give even more power to senators who represent a small fraction of the nation. A Senate rule passed in 1917 allows any one senator to continue debate on a bill indefinitely, stalling a vote, until three-fifths of senators vote to end debate. Senators use this threat of endless debate, called a filibuster, to make it really hard to pass legislation, even popular legislation. Because of the threat of a filibuster, a simple majority of votes, 51 out of 100, is not good enough to pass a law. Bills need a supermajority, 60 out of 100 votes, to even have a chance. "The filibuster allows lawmakers elected by *less than* 17 percent of voters to exercise veto power over any and all laws," writes Eric Levitz in *New York* magazine. "This is a monstrously anti-democratic institution with no parallel in any other advanced democracy."

The perplexing question is what to do about the Senate. Changing the composition of the Senate requires not only a constitutional amendment—but also for every single state to agree. That's because Article V of the Constitution reads that "no State, without its Consent, shall be deprived of its equal Suffrage in the Senate."

Some proposals include large states breaking into multiple smaller states that would have two senators each. "A Democracy Restoration Act could grant blanket consent to populous but underrepresented states to go forth and multiply to restore the Senate's democratic legitimacy," says Burt Neuborne, professor of law at New York University. But this would require citizens in large states to agree to the fracturing of their states.

Political scientist Matthew Shugart of the University of

California, Davis, offers this idea, inspired by the Australian Senate: Increase the size of the Senate from 100 members to 150, 200, or 250. Each state would still get the same number of senators as required by the Constitution—three each, four each, or five each depending on the size of the senate. Voters would elect their senators all at the same time using proportional representation.

In other words, if each state had three senators, and 60 percent of voters in a state supported Democratic candidates and 40 percent supported Republicans, that state's new senators would be the top two Democratic candidates and the top Republican. "These changes would make the Senate more representative of the people without depriving any state of equal representation," Shugart says. "Instead of Republican states and Democratic states, each state would likely be represented by senators from both parties—and maybe even a third party—reducing polarization."

The filibuster problem has an easier fix. All it would take is a majority of senators agreeing to change the rule. "The filibuster is not in the Constitution," says Chris Weigant, a political commentator. "It is merely a tactic the Senate has gotten used to using, which means it can be changed at any time."

Some members of Congress want change. They are working to create a bipartisan Joint Committee on the Congress of Tomorrow that will propose improvements to the rules, procedures, and structures of the Congress. Learn more at www .conginst.org/congressional-reform-project.

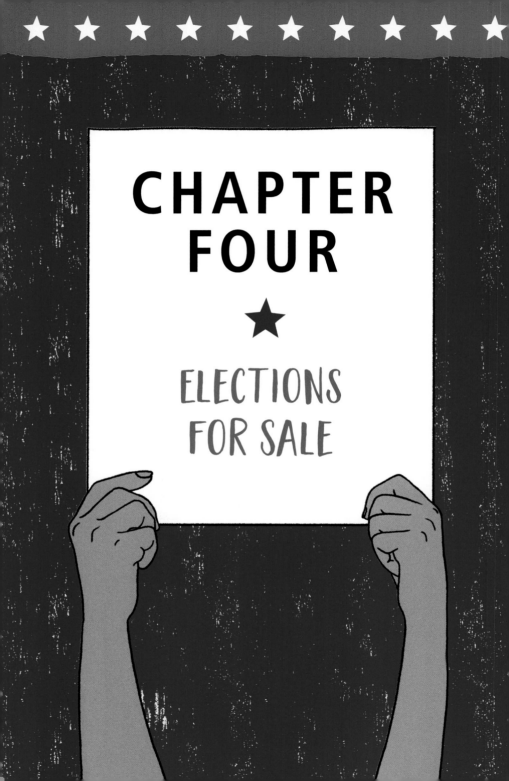

It's time to terminate gerrymandering.

Arnold Schwarzenegger (R), former governor of California

Partisan gerrymanders are incompatible with democratic principles.

—Supreme Court Justice Ruth Bader Ginsburg, appointed by President Bill Clinton (D)

[Gerrymandering] is cancerous, undermining the fundamental tenets of our form of democracy.

—Federal judge Paul Niemeyer, appointed by President George H.W. Bush (R)

Americans deserve better. Congressional representation should not be a political blood sport that protects incumbents, disenfranchises legitimate interests, and allows people to achieve with surgical reappointment what they couldn't do honestly at the ballot box.

—Oregon member of congress Earl Blumenauer (D)

CHAPTER THREE

★ FLASH ★

UNREPRESENTATIVE SENATE

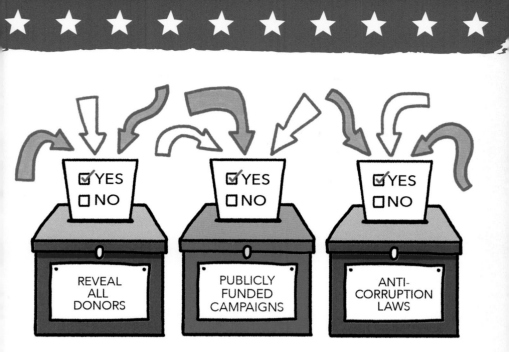

YES ☑ / NO ☐ — REVEAL ALL DONORS
YES ☑ / NO ☐ — PUBLICLY FUNDED CAMPAIGNS
YES ☑ / NO ☐ — ANTI-CORRUPTION LAWS

THE VAST MAJORITY OF AMERICANS, EIGHT OUT OF TEN, THINK MONEY HAS TOO MUCH INFLUENCE IN POLITICS.

I n 2014, voters in Rialto, California, received mailers from a group called Californians for Good Schools and Good Jobs. The organization opposed a local ballot measure that would raise taxes on oil companies. Guess who put up the $38,000 to pay for the mailer? An oil company. The tax measure failed by just 1,154 votes. Defeating it saved the company, Phillips 66, more than *4 billion.*

In the same year, a group called Carolina Rising spent $5 million on a three-month ad blitz in support of Thom Tillis's campaign for senator (R-NC). Almost all of the funding— 99 percent—came from one donor. But the donor who helped Tillis win the seat remains a secret.

In 2017, Doug Deason, a wealthy Texas donor, threatened to "close the Dallas piggy bank" which funded candidates unless Republican lawmakers delivered policies he and his friends wanted. "Get Obamacare repealed and replaced, get tax reform passed," he said. "You control the Senate. You control the House. You have the presidency. There's no reason you can't get this done. Get it done and we'll open it back up."

The vast majority of Americans, eight out of ten, think money has too much influence in politics. It's scary to realize how right they are.

In 2014, two political scientists, Martin Gilens of Princeton University and Benjamin I. Page of Northwestern University, asked a simple question: *Does the government pass laws that Americans want?* After studying twenty years of public opinion polls and policies to see how responsive our government is to the will of the people, they came to a sobering conclusion: Whether or not most Americans supported an idea did not affect the likelihood that Congress would pass the law. "The preferences of the average American appear to have only a minuscule, near-zero, statistically non-significant impact upon public policy," they wrote.

If average Americans aren't influencing lawmakers, who is? Rich donors and corporations, that's who. "The central point that emerges from our research," Gilens and Page wrote, "is that economic elites and organized groups

GOVERNMENT BY THE WEALTHY

Martin Gilens of Princeton University and Benjamin I. Page of Northwestern University reviewed twenty years of public opinion surveys and the laws that were passed to see if what Americans wanted became law. These graphs compare the ideal where our government is responsive to the will of the people and the reality: Only the opinions of wealthy Americans matter.

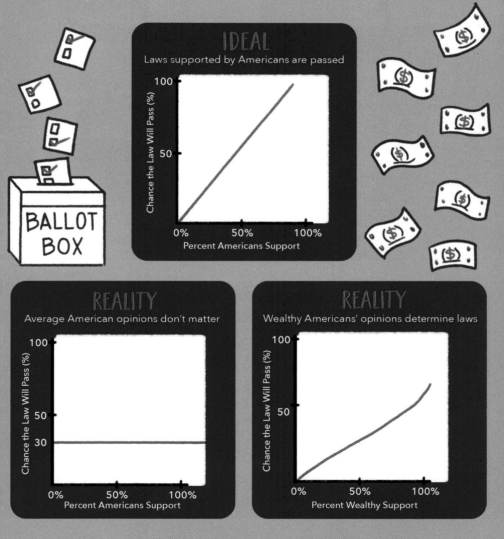

Source: Martin Gilens of Princeton University and Benjamin I. Page of Northwestern University and RepresentUs

representing business interests have substantial independent impacts on U.S. government policy."

Is this how our democracy is supposed to work?

MONEY TALKS

It costs money to run for office—to hire staff, set up a website,
pay for advertising, and hold town halls and rallies. Gathering signatures and supporters for a ballot initiative can cost a
lot too. Money for these efforts comes from multiple sources:
candidates' personal funds, small and large donations from
individuals, grants from political parties, and donations from
other organizations.

People donate to campaigns as a way of boosting the candidates, ideas, and policies they support. But while many Americans can't afford to make any political contributions and some
support their favorite candidates through small donations, the
richest Americans have the ability to pour in millions. That
much money can swing elections and ultimately affect government programs, regulations, and other laws.

Even though fewer than one in three Americans polled
by Quinnipiac University supported the 2017 tax cut, Rep.
Chris Collins (R-N.Y.) felt great pressure from contributors
to his campaign to pass the legislation. "My donors are
basically saying, 'Get it done or don't ever call me again.'"
The tax cut passed. Norm Ornstein, a policy expert at the
conservative American Enterprise Institute, called the bill

"a great big wet kiss—and in this case, not one that was uninvited—to big donors."

Former Georgia senator William Wyche Fowler (D) explains being beholden to donors this way: "The brutal fact that we all agonize over is that if you get two calls and one is from a constituent who wants to complain about the VA mistreating her father . . . and one is from somebody who is going to give you a party and raise $10,000, you call back the contributor. There's no way to justify it. Except that you rationalize that you have to have money or you can't campaign."

WHAT IS LEGAL?

Federal laws, state laws, and Supreme Court rulings have created a patchwork of guidelines governing spending on elections. It can be dizzying for citizens to figure out who is allowed to donate, how much money, to whom, when, and for what purpose.

There are two main kinds of campaign spending. First, candidates collect money and spend it to run their campaigns. Second, there are outside groups, unaffiliated with a campaign, that buy advertising and spend money in other ways to support or oppose candidates or ballot initiatives.

Donations *directly to campaigns* are limited by federal and state laws. Federal laws prohibit corporations, unions, government contractors, and noncitizens from donating to federal campaigns—and limit individual spending to $2,800 per candidate per election. More than half the states allow some level of corporate and union contributions directly to state candidates. Four states (Missouri, Oregon, Utah, and Virginia) have no individual limits at all for donations to state candidates.

In the 2016 presidential and congressional elections, *outside spending* accounted for $1.4 billion of the $6.4 billion total, according to the nonpartisan Center for Responsive Politics. This money is supposed to be collected and spent by people or groups not directly involved in campaigns. But in practice, these funds are often raised by people with connections to candidates and campaigns, including family members and former campaign staff. Much of this spending is unlimited—and worse, some is secret. This secret funding is often called dark money.

Here's how it works. Almost anyone can create a political action committee (PAC) by filing some paperwork and opening a bank account. A popular version is a super PAC. Super PACs can't contribute to or coordinate directly with campaigns, but they can buy ads, send mailings (like the mailer sent by Californians for Good Schools and Good Jobs), or otherwise promote or undermine a specific candidate or ballot measure. Any person, corporation, union, or other group can contribute *unlimited* money to these efforts. So while it is illegal for someone to make a $3,000 contribution directly to a candidate, the same person can contribute *$3 million* to a super PAC's ad campaign to support the same candidate.

It's also completely legal to keep the origin of the $3 million donation secret. This happens through two categories of nonprofits. "Social welfare" organizations, such as the AARP

WHO GIVES MONEY?

48%
Large Donors

11%
Small Donors

13%
Self-Financing

28%
Political Action Committees

Source: Center for Responsive Politics and the Federal Election Commission, 2018

(formerly the American Association of Retired Persons), the National Rifle Association (NRA), and Planned Parenthood Action Fund, can spend up to *half* of their budgets on political activities—and they don't have to reveal their donors.

The other secretive groups are the "trade associations," such as Pharmaceutical Research and Manufacturers of America (PhRMA), the American Petroleum Institute (API), and the American Chemical Association. These groups of American and multinational companies can spend *unlimited amounts of money* on political activities, without reporting their donors.

What does all this mean? Corporations and individuals can spend *unlimited* amounts on political efforts separate from

ALL ABOUT MONEY

Campaign finance: How elections are funded.

Campaign spending: Donations to and spending by candidates.

Outside spending: Funds spent on political efforts separate from candidates' campaigns.

Dark money: Political spending meant to influence voters where the source of the funding is secret.

Social-welfare group: Tax-exempt nonprofits that can use up to half of their funds on political activities. These organizations can spend unlimited funds separate from candidates' campaigns and do not have to disclose their donors.

Trade association: A group of companies in the same industry that develop and promote the industry. These tax-exempt nonprofits can spend unlimited funds separate from candidates' campaigns and do not have to disclose the donors.

PAC: Political action committee. A PAC can donate $5,000 to a candidate's campaign.

Super PAC: Can receive and spend unlimited amounts of money separate from a candidate's campaign. Super PACs must reveal the organizations that donated to them—but not the names of people who funded those organizations.

Public financing: When candidates get some or all of the money for their campaigns from public funds.

Small donations: Donations of $200 or less.

Lobbyist: A person who tries to convince government officials to change laws.

campaigns, legally. They can secretly donate as much as they want to these nonprofits, legally. The nonprofits can donate as much as they want to super PACs, which must disclose the name of the nonprofit—but not the original donors.

Welcome to the wild world of "dark" or hidden money.

A Brennan Center report found that as much as 70 percent of "outside" spending is hidden. "In my 33 years in Arizona politics and government, dark money is the most corrupting influence I have seen," says former legislator and political analyst Chris Herstam, who has served as both a Republican and a Democrat.

ONE PERSON
(WITH ENOUGH MONEY) CAN SPEND:

★ $2,800 on each federal candidate per election

★ $5,000 to any political action committee per year

★ $10,000 total to state and local parties per year

★ $35,500 on a national political party per year

★ *Unlimited amount* to their own campaign

★ *Unlimited amount* to super PACs

★ *Unlimited amount*, secretly, to "social welfare" and trade association groups

Spending limits on contributions to state-level candidates vary by state.

WHAT DARK MONEY CAN DO

James Bennet recalls watching TV with his brother Michael, who was running for U.S. Senate in Colorado in 2010. The airwaves were filled with political ads, their funding unknown. "His image was distorted, the voice-overs were ominous, and all in all, the ads made him seem like a devil," he recalls. "In between the ads attacking my brother, I saw ads doing the same thing to his opponent and to candidates in other races."

Hidden donors have no incentive to be truthful or respectful in their attacks on opponents. Negative, false political ads fill our screens. In 2018, one false ad claimed that Jared Polis (D), a candidate for governor, wanted Colorado schools to be put under Islamic Sharia law. Another ad doctored a photo of Georgia candidate Stacey Abrams (D) to make it look like she was a communist.

Michael Sargeant of the Democratic Legislative Campaign Committee describes dark money this way: "Instead of being in a boxing match in a ring, you're in a dark alley being hit by four or five people, and you don't know who they are." People viewing these ads also have no idea where the money for them originates.

Dark money packs a powerful punch at the state and local level, according to research by the Brennan Center. "For a relative pittance—less than $100,000—corporations and others can use dark money to shape the outcome of a low-level race in which they have a direct stake," says the Brennan Center's

Chisun Lee. State and local ballot measures also attract lots of dark money, like the California oil company tax measure. "Dark money is most likely to turn up where the stakes are particularly valuable, in amounts that could make all the difference in persuading voters," the Brennan Center's report says.

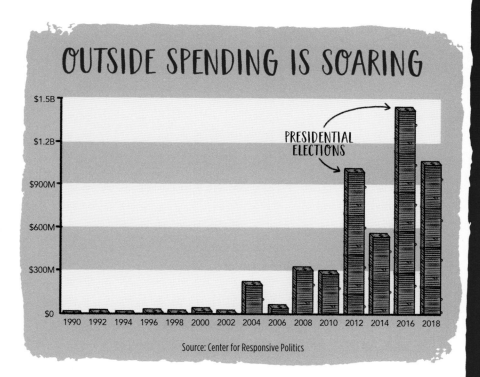

OUTSIDE SPENDING IS SOARING

PRESIDENTIAL ELECTIONS

Source: Center for Responsive Politics

HIDDEN DONORS HAVE NO INCENTIVE
TO BE TRUTHFUL OR RESPECTFUL IN
THEIR ATTACKS ON OPPONENTS.

FOREIGN INFLUENCE?

Seventy-eight percent of voters believe foreigners influence American elections "very often" or "somewhat often." They may be right. Currently, dark money from other countries can legally enter our elections through individual and corporate donations to social welfare organizations and trade associations—and through the internet.

Trevor Potter, of the Campaign Legal Center, says: "The door to secret foreign dollars in U.S. elections remains wide open through secret contributions to these ostensibly 'nonpolitical' groups [social welfare organizations] that run campaign ads without any disclosure of their donors." Fred Wertheimer, of the campaign reform group Democracy 21, warns: "There is no way to determine if [a social welfare] group that is spending money to influence federal elections is taking that money from Russia, from Russian agents, from China or from any other foreign interest." Without stricter disclosure laws there is no way to know.

Trade associations, some with dues as high as $20 million a year, retain numerous foreign corporations as members. One of the top donors to the American Petroleum Institute (API), through a U.S. subsidiary, is Aramco, an oil company owned by the Saudi Arabian government. SABIC, a Saudi-owned chemical company, is a dues-paying member of the American Chemical Council, as are Solvay SA, a Belgian company, and Daikin Industries of Japan.

Foreign corporations that want to affect policy can also just buy a U.S. company. "Think of Burger King, which merged with Tim Horton's and is now Canadian," says Ciara Torres-Spelliscy, professor of law at Stetson University and the author of *Corporate Citizen: An Argument for the Separation of Corporation and State.* "Nestle USA is operated by Nestle SA, which is headquartered in Switzerland. 7-Eleven is owned by a Japanese company. Firestone is owned by Bridgestone, which is also Japanese. The Pierre Hotel in New York City is owned by an Indian conglomerate called the Tata Group." And all these U.S. subsidiaries can spend unlimited amounts on U.S. elections—in the open or secretly through trade associations and social welfare organizations.

Then there is the internet. In 2016, 11.4 million Americans saw paid political ads on Facebook created and paid for by Russian people and companies. More than 16 million Americans on Instagram also saw Russian-backed political content. A Russian state-controlled news network's paid tweets appeared in approximately 54 million user feeds.

For the most part, no one knew about it. That's because there is currently no law requiring disclosure of the source of political ads online—foreign or otherwise. "Regardless of whether it affected the outcome of the election," says a report by the Brennan Center, "the Kremlin's activity represents a threat to national security and popular sovereignty—the exercise of the American people's power to decide the course their government takes."

THE PROBLEM WITH LOBBYISTS

People and organizations can also influence policy through lobbying. The term *lobbyist* comes from the fact that many people are not allowed to enter legislative chambers; in the early days, people who wanted to talk with legislators about issues or policies often hung out in the lobby to catch officials in transit.

There is nothing wrong with lobbying a member of Congress, state legislator, or other public official about issues you care about. In fact, it's a great way for them to learn what their voters want and why. It is also a constitutionally protected right of free speech mentioned in the First Amendment as "the right to petition the government for redress of grievances." The problem comes when there is money in the mix.

Professional lobbyists are hired by wealthy individuals or corporations to influence public officials. They not only discuss bills with legislators and draft legislation, but also personally contribute to campaigns (subject to the same limits as everyone else) and outside spending efforts (without limit). They gain even more influence by acting as fundraisers, gathering contributions for politicians in the hopes of winning political favors. Professional lobbyists sometimes even offer public officials high-paying jobs after they leave office, where

THE 200 MOST POLITICALLY ACTIVE COMPANIES SPENT $5.8 BILLION INFLUENCING OUR GOVERNMENT—EARNING A RETURN OF 750 TIMES THEIR INVESTMENT.

they earn their salary by influencing their former colleagues. And all of this is legal.

The nonpartisan group RepresentUs calls this the vicious cycle of legalized corruption. Say a wealthy person or corporation wants a law passed, revoked, or changed. They hire a team of lobbyists to make their case to legislators. But it doesn't stop there. The lobbyists also make contributions to candidates, to political parties, and—without limit—to outside groups that support the candidates they target. The elected officials get the law passed and are regaled with more donations and gifts while in office, and lucrative lobbying jobs when their terms are up.

RepresentUs found that "in the last 5 years alone, the 200 most politically active companies in the U.S. spent $5.8 billion influencing our government with lobbying and campaign contributions. Those same companies got $4.4 trillion in taxpayer support—earning a return of 750 times their investment."

ONE PERCENTERS FUND CAMPAIGNS

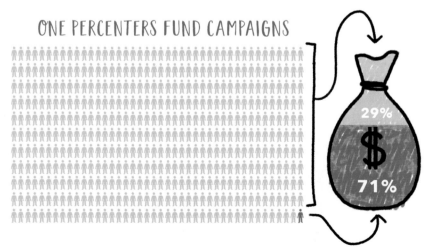

In 2018, 99.5 percent of Americans contributed less than $200 each to political campaigns. A tiny elite, just a half of a percent of Americans, funded 71 percent of contributions to Congress.

Source: Center for Responsive Politics

THE WISHES OF THE WEALTHY

We have to ask ourselves: Do we want to be governed by and for corporations and the extremely rich? What corporations want can be quite different from what average Americans need. For instance, many Americans struggle to pay for costly prescription drugs. One way to bring down the cost is for the government program Medicare to negotiate with drug companies for lower prices. But the drug companies want to keep prices—and their profits—high. "Can anybody guess how much the big pharma industry spent on lobbying last year?" Danny O'Connor (D) asked voters in Ohio that question while campaigning for the U.S. House. "Two hundred and forty million. They all but pooh-poohed any legislation that would allow Medicare to negotiate prescription drug prices."

Recent studies comparing the priorities of the very rich to ordinary Americans also reveal stark differences. "Affluent Americans have substantially differing views on issues such as the minimum wage, the deficit, job creation, and criminal justice reform," states a report by the Brennan Center. Another study showed that almost 90 percent of average Americans are committed to excellence in public schools, compared to just 35 percent of the billionaire class. Billionaires are also much less supportive than most Americans of universal health care and financial help for unemployed people.

DO WE WANT TO BE GOVERNED BY AND FOR CORPORATIONS AND THE EXTREMELY RICH?

PRICED OUT OF PUBLIC SERVICE

All the money in politics also affects who can run for office. The cost of running a successful campaign has skyrocketed. This has tilted the system toward the rich, whether they be self-funding billionaires or simply those with the means to go without an income for a year or two while campaigning. It has put ordinary working people at a huge disadvantage. How could someone who struggles to support their family, has no extra money of their own to contribute, and no wealthy friends and family or other connections ever dream of running for public office?

Also, candidates who are not wealthy enough to underwrite their own campaigns must spend a large part of every day working to meet fundraising goals. To win a Senate seat in 2014, candidates had to raise $14,351 every single day.

MONEY WINS

AVERAGE MONEY SPENT

$23M

$1.1M

Winners **Losers**

CHANCE OF WINNING

Spent more
91%

9%
Spent less

Source: RepresentUs and the Federal Election Commission, 2012 and 2014

Frank Kovach has seen this even at the most local level. "Historically, for school board races, if you raised $10,000 or $12,000, that was a well-funded race," says the Republican who served on the Sarasota, Florida, school board for sixteen years. "Now all of a sudden you need $100,000 to run for school board."

Once on the fundraising treadmill, it's hard to step off. An Oklahoma State University study found that in more than 90 percent of congressional races, the candidate who raises the most money wins.

The influence of money and the growing competition for candidates to raise more and more of it distracts our officials from their most important duty: governing. Members of Congress can spend up to five hours a day fundraising for reelection—as much as or more than they spend legislating, according to one study. Without such a heavy fundraising burden, our representatives could be talking and listening to the people they represent, researching the issues, and working with others on solutions.

> **IN MORE THAN 90 PERCENT OF CONGRESSIONAL RACES, THE CANDIDATE WHO RAISES THE MOST MONEY WINS.**

NO-PAC PLEDGE

A growing number of candidates are doing what they can to take big money out of their own campaigns. In 2018, Dean Phillips (D-Minn.) refused to accept PAC money in his quest for a seat in

HOW BAD IS YOUR STATE?

States that allow people to give unlimited amounts of money to political candidates in the state

States that allow corporations to contribute to directly to state candidates

States that have no contribution limits at all for statewide campaigns

States with reasonable limits

Sources: National Conference of State Legislatures, Follow the Money, *The Oregonian*

VALE
KOCH INDUSTRIES
CHEVRON
WALMART
PFIZER
PILOT CORP GSK Wheatland Tube CONOCO
NEXTERA ENERGY DON McGILL PHILLIPS
ANDEAVOR Altria TOYOTA OF KATY PEABODY INVESTMENTS
EXXON TRT HOLLYWOOD AI Altep MARATHON
HOLDINGS DEVELOPMENT Holdings PETROLEUM

Source: Open Secrets

Congress. He raised $2.3 million, 99 percent from individuals—and won. Beto O'Rourke (D) raised $79 million in his run to unseat Senator Ted Cruz (R-Tex.) without accepting PAC money. "It's a major theme of the campaign," his communications director said. "People want to know that you are going to respond to them and their interests, and not the most recent check you received." O'Rourke lost, but he raised more than Cruz and came closer to winning than most people expected.

Fifty-two members of the 116th Congress have pledged to reject money from corporate PACs, including Francis Rooney (R-Fla.) and Phil Roe (R-Tenn.). Several presidential hopefuls for the 2020 election—Senator Cory Booker (D-N.J.), Senator Kamala Harris (D-Calif.), Senator Kirsten Gillibrand (D-N.Y.), Senator Bernie Sanders (I-Vt.), and Senator Elizabeth Warren (D-Mass.)—have all made no-corporate-PAC pledges.

WHAT AMERICANS WANT

Such pledges are catching voters' attention. Laurie Wolfe is liberal, and her two brothers are conservative. But they all support campaign finance reform–minded candidates. "We need to get rid of these politicians who only care about their corporate donors and getting reelected," she says. "A lot of people like us find it refreshing to have a candidate that's going to the people rather than the big donors."

In fact, three-quarters of voters, both Republicans and Democrats, say it's very important that major political donors don't have any more influence than the public. Similar numbers of voters want limits on outside spending for ads. Regarding those nonprofit "social welfare" groups that spend money on political activities, 76 percent of the public want them to disclose their donors, according to a *New York Times*/CBS News poll.

Spending limits is a thorny issue, but one that many committed activists are taking on. In the case *Citizens United v. FEC,* the U.S. Supreme Court ruled that outside political spending is a form of speech protected by the Constitution and that corporations and unions are entitled to the same free speech protections as people. Limiting outside spending for individuals, corporations, and unions will remain illegal until one of three things happens: The current Supreme Court justices change their minds, the composition of the court changes, or there is a widespread movement to support a constitutional amendment.

A number of groups, such as End Citizens United and Move to Amend, are doing just that. "No doubt it is ridiculously difficult to amend our Constitution," says Harvard Law School professor Lawrence Lessig. "The veto of one house in just 13 states—representing as little as 5 percent of the American public—could block an amendment. But in the last hundred years we've added 10 amendments to our Constitution . . . We've done it before; we can do it again."

The Supreme Court has stated that requiring disclosure is constitutional—and necessary. The *Citizens United* ruling stated: "Transparency enables the electorate to make informed decisions and give proper weight to different speakers and messages." In 2018, forty-two states considered bills on disclosure—and eighty-one bills were enacted. Reforms include requiring that anyone buying a political ad reveal their donors, for those donors to reveal who funded them, and for the top donors' names to appear on the ad.

> **BOTH REPUBLICANS AND DEMOCRATS SAY IT'S VERY IMPORTANT THAT MAJOR POLITICAL DONORS DON'T HAVE ANY MORE INFLUENCE THAN THE PUBLIC.**

PUBLICLY FUNDED CAMPAIGNS

There's another way to take government out of the hands of wealthy individuals and corporations: publicly funded campaigns. The United States currently has twenty-seven programs to publicly fund candidates. Fourteen of these programs are statewide. Many require candidates to collect a certain number of small donations (perhaps $5) from people in their district to show that they are legitimate candidates. Then they receive a set amount of public money to match or multiply the small donations they receive. New York City's eight-to-one match, for example, would turn a $100 donation into $800. Candidates in these voluntary programs may also be subject to spending limits.

In one innovative program, Seattle, Washington, provides four $25 vouchers to all registered voters. Voters can allocate the funding to the local candidates of their choice. "The promise of the vouchers is turning every single voter in the city into a donor," says Alan Durning of the northwest policy group Sightline Institute.

Public financing widens the pool of candidates who can run for state legislature, a number of studies have found. When Cicero Booker (I) decided to run for state senate from one of the poorest districts in Connecticut, most people in his community had never donated to a campaign. But when they heard that a $5 donation would help him qualify for public funding, the donations flowed in.

Publicly financed elections have allowed people with a wide array of jobs to run: "artists, administrative assistants, barbers and beauticians, cab and bus operators, carpenters, police officers, students, nurses, and clergy," according to the Brennan Center.

More diverse candidates run for office too. The Center for Governmental Studies found that while 16 percent of candidates in typical elections were people of color, they made up 30 percent of publicly funded candidates. "I didn't come from money," says state senator Gary A. Winfield (D-Conn.). "I am a candidate of color, and I wasn't a candidate for the political party or machine apparatus. I didn't have the nomination, and I was actually able to defeat the person that had the nomination by talking about issues that he wasn't. It not only leveled the playing field, it completely upended the playing field."

Andrew Hall, professor of political science at Stanford University, similarly found that challengers in publicly financed programs were able to mount more successful campaigns against incumbents.

Such programs also tend to shift dependency away from wealthy donors, according to a study by Public Campaign, a feature many candidates appreciate. Janet Napolitano (D), who ran for governor of Arizona with public financing, calls the program "the difference between being able to go out and spend your time talking with voters, meeting with groups, traveling to communities that have been underrepresented in the past, as opposed to being on the phone selling tickets to a $250 a plate fundraiser." One study found that the average state legislator whose campaign was publicly financed spent as little as 8 percent of his or her time fundraising.

Matt Lesser (D) thinks public financing has made him a more effective Maine legislator: "[The program] has made me directly accountable. It has made me earn people's support the hard way. And it has also helped me be a better candidate in the sense that I know what is on people's minds a heck of a lot better than if I had not had that experience to go out there, meet them, and listen to what their concerns are."

WIDESPREAD SUPPORT

Public funding for campaigns has helped both Republicans and Democrats, the research group Public Campaign found. The programs are popular with both parties, winning accolades from two-thirds of Democrats and Republicans.

They are popular with voters, too. In 2018, voters passed a slew of campaign finance reforms. Baltimore joined its neighbors in Montgomery Country, Prince Georges County, and Washington, D.C., in offering a public funding system. Denver voted in a small donation match program. And New Yorkers strengthened and updated their public funding of campaigns.

WHAT IN THE WORLD?

America's level of spending on elections is among the highest in the world. The price tag of U.S. elections dwarfs that of many other nations.

Part of the difference is that television advertising, the largest part of most U.S. election budgets, is handled differently in some other countries. Some countries ban political ads on television altogether while others offer small amounts of free and equal time to candidates.

Also, some countries—Austria, Hungary, Italy, New Zealand, Slovakia, and the United Kingdom—limit campaign spending. Others—Belgium, Canada, Chile, France, Greece, Iceland, Ireland, Israel, Japan, South Korea, Poland, and Slovenia—limit both contributions and spending.

The United States and Finland are the only countries that limit contributions but don't limit spending. Political commentator Paul Waldman calls this "the worst of both worlds."

"The lack of spending limits means [candidates] are always at risk of being outspent, which means they can never stop raising money," he says. "But contribution limits means they have to get that money in [small] increments, meaning they have to keep asking and asking and asking."

Elections in other parts of the world are heavily publicly financed. In Norway, for example, about three-quarters of funding comes from the government.

PUBLIC MONEY FOR PRESIDENTIAL CAMPAIGNS

Since 1976, the Presidential Election Campaign Fund has offered presidential candidates a public financing option. Citizens have the option of checking off a box on their income tax forms to donate $3 of their taxes to the fund. Once a candidate reaches a specified level of public support, they have access to matching funds and grants and are subject to spending limits.

The campaigns of Ronald Reagan (R), George H. W. Bush (R), Robert Dole (R), Jimmy Carter (D), and Bill Clinton (D) opted in to the program, agreed to spending limits, and received more than $20 million each. "The bottom line is this system did exactly what it was supposed to do for more than two decades," says Fred Wertheimer of the reform group Democracy 21. "The system was not perfect, but it allowed candidates to run competitive races for office. It kept the candidates away from private-influence money. It worked."

While the level of public funding has remained stagnant, campaign spending has exploded, and fewer candidates have embraced the program. That's because if one candidate has public funding with a spending cap and the opponent doesn't, they aren't on a level playing field. In 2000, George W. Bush (R) did not join the program until after the primary. In 2008, Barack Obama (D) first pledged to go the public funding route but reversed course and opted out. In 2016, only Democratic candidate Martin O'Malley participated.

Some members of Congress are working to update the program through the Empower Act. Citizens could check off a box on their tax returns to contribute $20 to the fund. Candidates who showed support in twenty states would get $6 in public funds for every dollar they raised in small donations. But they could accept only $1,000 maximum per person rather than the current cap of $2,800. "It's not just a matter of exhorting candidates to accept public financing," says U.S. Rep. David Price (D-N.C.). "It is also a matter of fixing the statute so that it is more in line with what a candidate . . . is going to need."

Congress is also considering other federal programs. Thirty senators have cosponsored the Fair Elections Now Act, for public funding of U.S. Senate races. And more than a hundred and fifty members of Congress have signed on to the Government by the People Act, which grants people a $25 My Voice tax credit to encourage political donations and would match small-dollar contributions at a six-to-one ratio.

Small donations can add up to big money. For example, Bernie Sanders's 2016 campaign for president collected roughly $120 million, the vast majority from donations of less than $200.

The U.S. Supreme Court has ruled that these programs are constitutional, stating that they do not "abridge, restrict, or censor speech," but instead "use public money to facilitate and enlarge public discussion and participation in the electoral process, goals vital to a self-governing people."

CITIZENS RISE UP

Many observers believe that true transformation requires citizens working at all levels to demand publicly funded elections, to require disclosure of all political contributions, and to pass measures that limit the influence of money. The Anti-Corruption Act, which the bipartisan group RepresentUs is pushing nationally and at state and local levels, requires online disclosure of all significant political fundraising and spending and of major donors for all political ads. The act bars politicians from raising money during the workday and from lobbying for several years after leaving office, and bars paid lobbyists from donating to politicians. Citizens have already passed more than ninety anticorruption acts in towns and cities, and even a few states, across the country.

> CITIZENS HAVE PASSED MORE THAN NINETY ANTICORRUPTION ACTS IN TOWNS, CITIES, AND STATES ACROSS THE COUNTRY.

Dina Butcher and Ellen Chaffee, self-described "badass grandmas" who support different political parties, led an effort to pass such a measure in North Dakota. "I feel strongly that our voices as citizens are not being heard as our democracy should dictate," says Butcher. "It's not that we've lost our way—we're losing our soul." Their amendment, which restricts gifts from lobbyists, bars foreign money in elections, and requires full disclosure of all political donations, passed in 2018 in their state.

Yours can too.

WHAT YOU CAN DO

RepresentUs brings progressive and conservative citizens together to pass laws that reduce the influence of money in your town, city, state, and country. Volunteer at a local chapter or check out a step-by-step guide to starting your own movement at represent.us.

Democracy Matters, a nonpartisan, nonprofit group, mobilizes students at more than thirty-six campuses nationwide in support of publicly funded elections. To find or start a chapter, visit www.democracymatters.org/about-us/campus-s.

Take Back Our Republic offers conservative solutions to campaign finance. Learn more and support their work at TakeBack.org.

End Citizens United is a PAC organized to reform campaign finance. To volunteer on reform efforts, check out endcitizensunited.org/action-center.

Sign a petition and encourage your state and federal representatives to pass the "We the People Amendment," which declares that money is not speech, corporations are not people, and the campaign finance restrictions are legal, at www.movetoamend.org.

FOR MORE INFORMATION

The National Institute of Money in Politics offers a free public database where you can search political contributions and campaign finance efforts nationwide or statewide. Before voting, check where the candidates get their money. Go to www.followthemoney.org.

The National Conference of State Legislatures tracks spending limits, disclosure laws, and public financing laws in all fifty states. Find out what your state does and does not do to limit the influence of money in government at www.cfinst .org/law/stateLinks.aspx.

Campaign finance is like the gateway issue to
every other issue that you might care about—whether
it be education or tax reform or foreign policy.

—ANN M. RAVEL (D), FORMER CHAIR OF THE FEDERAL ELECTION COM-
MISSION, WHICH OVERSEES ELECTION FINANCE LAWS

Virtually everybody in the Senate is in favor of enhanced disclosure, greater disclosure; that's hardly a controversial subject.

—U.S. SENATOR MITCH MCCONNELL (R-KY.)

Money's dominance over politics is a top problem our
nation faces. It prevents us from tackling anything else.
We have reached a stunning point: Either we are a country
that makes decisions based on the common good, or one
where the size of your wallet determines the worth of
your ideas. Either we uphold the values of a representative democracy or we allow greed and wealth to destroy
the great American experiment in self-governance.

—FORMER U.S. SENATOR ALAN SIMPSON (R-WYO.)

If we build a new system that makes everyday Americans just
as powerful as the big money crowd, we can ensure that the priorities and concerns of the people will once again find expres-
sion in the public policy that comes out of Washington.

—U.S. REPRESENTATIVE JOHN SARBANES (D-MD.)

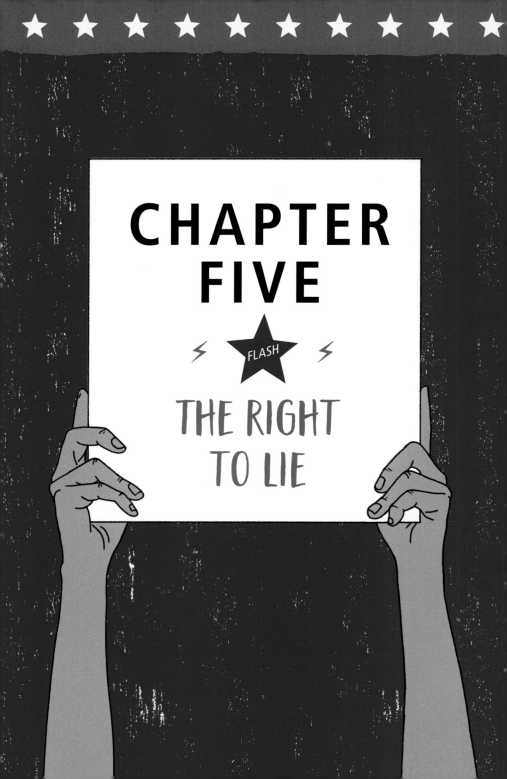

S ome politicians and campaigns lie. Political TV ads, leaflets stuffed in our mailboxes, and robocalls on our phones often contain lies. It's one reason Americans are exasperated, distrustful, and fed up with our democracy.

In the 2016 presidential campaign, PolitiFact, a nonpartisan, not-for-profit, fact-checking group, found that *25 percent* of Hillary Clinton's claims and *70 percent* of Donald Trump's were mostly or completely false.

Lies on the campaign trail happen at the state and local levels as well. Stacey Abrams (D), a 2018 candidate for Georgia governor, believes that only U.S. citizens should be allowed to vote, but a TV ad run by the Republican Party stated: "Abrams will let illegal immigrants vote." Illinois state senate candidate Barrett Davie (R) is vocally pro-choice, but a social media ad run by a political action committee that supported his opponent claimed: "Barrett Davie wants to take away a woman's right to make her own choice."

Political candidates, political parties, and political action committees can lie about anything they want. They can lie about candidates' voting records. They can lie about candidates' positions on issues. They can even lie about how a law or policy will affect people.

And here's the shocker—all these lies are perfectly legal.

Political ads—whether on TV, in your mailbox, or on the internet—are considered free speech protected by the First Amendment. "The theory is that government punishment of political speech is so dangerous to democracy and so vulnerable to abuse that we have to rely on citizens, and on political rivals, to determine the truth for themselves," says Rebecca Tushnet, a professor of First Amendment law at Georgetown Law School.

But does the process work? Candidates try to defend themselves against lies. Journalists and fact checkers try to correct the record, but "the political process cannot be counted on to smoke out lies and punish," says David Schultz, a professor of political science at Hamline University and the University of Minnesota Law School. "Moreover, once lies have been circulated, especially in a social media era, they are hard to correct, and evidence suggests deception travels more quickly and deeper than the truth."

You might think it's impossible to outlaw lying. After all, the First Amendment of the Constitution states, "Congress shall make no law . . . abridging the freedom of speech." But perjury—lying under oath—is illegal, with liars facing grave consequences. Corporations are not allowed to lie to manipulate stock prices and any that do face serious sanctions.

Furthermore, the federal government, through the Federal Trade Commission, already regulates speech in ads and requires truth in advertising. As the FTC website states: "When consumers see or hear an advertisement, whether it's on the Internet, radio or television, or anywhere else, federal law says that ad must be truthful, not misleading, and, when appropriate, backed by scientific evidence. The Federal Trade Commission enforces these truth-in-advertising laws, and it applies the same standards no matter where an ad appears—in newspapers and magazines, online, in the mail, or on billboards or buses."

These truth in advertising laws are strictly enforced. "When the FTC finds a case of fraud perpetrated on consumers," the website states, "the agency files actions in federal district court for immediate and permanent orders to stop scams, prevent fraudsters from perpetrating scams in the future; freeze their assets; and get compensation for victims."

When Kellogg falsely claimed that Frosted Mini-Wheats boosted attentiveness and Rice Krispies improved immunity, the Federal Trade Commission ordered Kellogg to stop the ads. Kellogg paid $15 million in settlements for related lawsuits. When the ride-share app Uber falsely advertised on its website that the company provided "the safest rides on the road," it had to pay a $10 million settlement in California. And Red Bull's unproven claim that drinking its beverage enhanced reaction time and concentration cost them $13 million in a class-action lawsuit.

Why do we have the right to know the truth about cereals, energy drinks, and corporate profits but not about the people representing us? And why are we protected from false claims made by ride-sharing companies but not by candidates running for office, the policies they support, and how those policies might affect us?

The double standard for commercial and political ads makes it even harder for voters to know what to believe. "You hear people say, 'The ads must have some truth to them, or they wouldn't let them on television,'" says Brooks Jackson of the Annenberg Public Policy Center at the University of Pennsylvania about lies in political ads. But broadcasters are actually required to run political ads, even if they know they include lies.

What can be done? "A good argument can be made that there is no constitutional right to lie," says Schultz of Hamline University and the University of Minnesota Law School. He points to a 1995 case, *McIntyre v. Ohio Elections Commission.* The U.S. Supreme Court ruled that deception is not protected by the First Amendment and that Ohio had a legitimate interest in preventing false statements that might have "serious adverse consequences." The integrity of elections was deemed a good enough reason for the state to prevent fraud in campaigns. "Prohibiting lying actually enhances robust debate and democracy," says Schultz.

But then in 2014, in *Susan B. Anthony List v. Driehaus,* the courts struck down an Ohio state law that prohibited politicians from making false statements during political campaigns. This more recent ruling discourages states from outlawing political lies.

Americans want the truth, especially from public officials. A poll conducted by the Association of Young Americans and the American Association of Retired Persons found that 86 percent of boomers, Gen Xers, and millennials believe honesty in government is essential to the future of our country.

There is nothing stopping states and the federal government from continuing to pass laws limiting political lies. Given the most recent court rulings, lawsuits will likely challenge these laws. But such efforts might eventually convince the courts that states, the federal government, and the people of the United States have a compelling interest in preserving honesty in politics.

Until then, it is up to voters to call out the lies and vote accordingly.

WHAT YOU CAN DO

Learn the Truth

Find the facts on current issues at the FactChecker: www.washingtonpost.com/news/fact-checker/?utm_term=.ee23150e4964.

Don't Spread Lies

Look out for and counter false stories that have gone viral on FactCheck's Facebook Initiative (www.factcheck.org/fake-news) and Viral Spiral project (www.factcheck.org/hot-topics).

Don't Vote for a Liar

PolitiFact tracks the truthfulness of many politicians and organizations. Before you vote, check the candidates' records and the records of organizations that support them and put out attack ads against their opponents: www.politifact.com/personalities.

Call Out the Lie

You can also call or email representatives to express dismay at their lies and write letters to the editor to expose lies you discover.

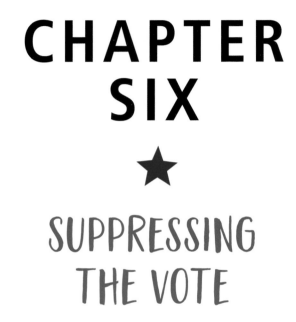

CHAPTER SIX

★

SUPPRESSING THE VOTE

In 2015, navy veteran Larry Harmon went to vote on a ballot measure, but was turned away. Poll workers said he was not registered. That made no sense to him. He had voted in Ohio before and he hadn't moved. What happened? Turns out that in 2012, he didn't like any of the presidential candidates so he didn't cast a ballot. For missing that election, the state purged his name from the rolls.

When New Jersey citizen Roslyn Wilson was ninety-seven, she feared she might never get to vote again. Usually, she and other elderly residents of her twelve-story apartment complex rode the elevator to vote at the polling place inside the building. But election officials planned to close that polling place. "Few of us have cars," says Wilson. "We'd have to walk, which a lot of people can hardly do, or take a bus. Many people would have just not voted."

Texan Sammie Bates wasn't allowed to vote until she saved up the $42 it cost to order the birth certificate she needed to get the ID her state required. Money was tight, so it took a while. "You're going to put money where you feel the need is most urgent," she says. "We couldn't eat the birth certificate and we couldn't pay rent with the birth certificate."

NEW VOTING LAWS BLOCK *MILLIONS* OF AMERICANS FROM VOTING.

Harmon, Wilson, and Bates are all victims of a phenomenon called voter suppression. In the last decade, about half of states passed new laws that created barriers to voting—that's right, new laws that make it harder for citizens to participate in democracy. These laws improperly purge voters from the rolls. They eliminate or reduce early voting and close popular polling places. Or they restrict voting by requiring IDs that many people don't have or can't afford. Though these changes seem small, in practice they block *millions* of fellow Americans from voting.

VOTER PURGES

Teresa Sharp, age fifty-two, had been voting since she was eighteen. She had lived in the same house outside Cincinnati for more than thirty years. So she was shocked to receive a letter stating: "You are hereby notified that your right to vote has been challenged by a qualified elector . . . The Hamilton County Board of Elections has scheduled a hearing . . . You have the right to appear, testify, call witnesses and be represented by council."

To Sharp, voting is "sacred, like my children," she says.

States regularly update voter rolls when people die or move out of the state. But that process can be abused. Sharp was swept up in an aggressive purge in Ohio, where more than 2 million voters were struck from the rolls. Ohio's software flagged Sharp's household as an "electoral irregularity" because it had six or more registered voters. But there is nothing irregular about living with other voters, especially for many low-income people, students, and those living with extended families.

REQUIRE THE RIGHT SYSTEM

Software used to purge rolls can be overly aggressive and discriminatory. For instance, the Interstate Crosscheck System—used by many states to identify people registered in more than one state—returns two hundred false positives for every double registration identified. Double registration doesn't mean much either. Voters often move and simply vote in their new state. There's little evidence of people with two registrations voting twice.

But we can keep our voter rolls clean and fair. Created with help from the Pew Charitable Trusts and used by fifteen states and growing, the Electronic Registration and Information Compact allows states to share voter and motor vehicle registrations, Postal Service addresses, and social security death records to fairly and accurately clean up their voter lists. Encourage your state to join. Visit www .ericstates.org.

Sharp traveled to the Board of Elections with six family members where she learned that her house was described as a vacant lot—by a citizen purging voter rolls who had never visited the street. Sharp was outraged.

While keeping the voter rolls accurate and updated makes good sense, "People have other things to do with their lives than respond to inaccurate complaints accusing them of being criminals," says Justin Levitt, professor at Loyola Law School in Los Angeles.

This is not a small, local problem, according to a report by the Brennan Center, which studied purges in forty-nine states. The authors state: "We found that between 2014 and 2016, states removed almost 16 million voters from the rolls, and every state in the country can and should do more to protect voters from improper purges."

REDUCING ACCESS TO POLLING PLACES

From 2013 to 2018, roughly a thousand polling places were closed, forcing voters to travel farther and wait in longer lines to vote. Other polling places have been moved to locations that are difficult for voters to reach. In 2018, the thirteen thousand registered voters in Dodge City, Kansas, many of them Latinx, had to leave the city to vote. Election officials had moved their one polling place to the suburbs.

Having to vote in an unfamiliar location keeps people from voting, a 2011 study found. Although election officials usually cite cutting costs, observers worry that closing and moving polling places is becoming a tool to shape the outcome of elections. Election officials can reduce the turnout in targeted areas by cutting polling places, or increase participation by opening polling places near supporters. "You can basically lessen the turnout of people who disagree with your position," says Abraham Rutchick, a psychology professor at California State University, Northridge, who studies polling placement.

Closing polling places can tip elections, says Nina Kohn, a law professor at Syracuse University. "This is not just an issue of fairness; it could affect tight races," she says. "It could be the difference between someone winning or someone losing."

LIMITS ON EARLY VOTING

For decades, recognizing that voters lead busy lives, states increased access by offering early voting. Early voting makes casting a ballot possible for many people—those who work or are in school, who care for young children, who care for the elderly, or who don't have cars or other easy transportation to the polls. Early voting gives them more flexibility to make any arrangements needed to get to the polls. In the 2012 presidential election, one in three Americans voted before Election Day.

But that has shifted since 2011, when state after state began slashing early voting, especially weekend and evening hours popular with people of color and hourly workers. Wisconsin cut early voting from thirty to twelve days—and limited the number of early voting sites to one per county.

Early voting is not offered equally even within the same state. In 2018, Damon Johnson, a busy nineteen-year-old studying chemical engineering at Prairie View A&M University, hoped to be able to vote early at a polling place on campus. "If I'm not eating or sleeping or studying, I'm really in class or in a meeting," he says. That's why he was dismayed to learn that election officials had restricted early voting at his historically black college to two days while the historically white Texas A&M nearby offered two weeks of early voting.

Cuts to early voting make Election Day more difficult. After Florida cut a week of early voting, more than two hundred thousand citizens were deterred from voting by long lines on Election Day. In 2016, MIT political scientist Charles Stewart led a survey of more than ten thousand voters in all fifty states about their recent election experiences. Roughly one in five waited in line for ten to thirty minutes.

BY ELIMINATING EARLY VOTING, STATES MAKE ELECTION DAY PARTICIPATION MORE DIFFICULT.

CAN I SEE YOUR ID?

States have erected another barrier to voting: IDs. Requiring voters to produce identification seems like common sense. In fact, the Help America Vote Act, passed by Congress in 2002, requires first-time voters to provide the last four digits of their social security number or their driver's license number, or show one of a number of IDs including a utility bill or paycheck. Federal voter registration forms also require voters to confirm that they are U.S. citizens and reside at their registered address.

While the federal government has deemed this sufficient, a number of states are greatly narrowing the list of approved ID options, making it much more difficult for many people to vote.

What could possibly be wrong with requiring a specific identification, such as a state-issued photo ID, to vote? A surprising number of voters don't have the required documentation. If you don't drive, don't have a credit card, and don't buy booze, you don't have much need for a photo ID. According to the Brennan Center, about 11 percent of Americans do not have state-issued photo IDs. That means more than *18 million* eligible voters don't own the identification required to vote in many states. Take Texas. In 2013, when the state instituted its voter ID law, an estimated *1.4 million voters* did not have the right ID.

University of Wisconsin–Madison political scientist Kenneth Mayer wondered what impact his state's new ID law had on voters. So he surveyed registered voters who did not cast ballots. More than 10 percent cited the fact that they didn't own the required ID. "We have hard evidence that there were tens of thousands of people who were unable to vote because of the voter ID law," he says. Likewise, the U.S. Government Accountability Office found that strict voter ID laws in Kansas and Tennessee decreased turnout by 2 to 3 percent.

For many people, it's neither free nor easy to get a state-issued photo ID. In Indiana, if you happen to have a current driver's license or passport with a name that perfectly matches the name on your voter registration form, you are all set. Everyone else has to go to the Bureau of Motor Vehicles to get an ID. But if you don't have a driver's license, you can't drive there. Many people in rural Indiana have no access to public transportation—and yet their motor vehicle department may be many miles away.

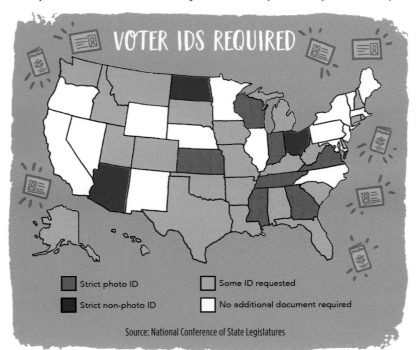

VOTER IDS REQUIRED

Strict photo ID

Strict non-photo ID

Some ID requested

No additional document required

Source: National Conference of State Legislatures

WHAT IN THE WORLD?

No other democracy restricts voting to people with government-issued photo IDs unless those IDs are widely and freely offered to all eligible citizens, according to research published in the *Harvard Law & Policy Review*. Australia, Denmark, New Zealand, and the United Kingdom do not require any identification, lead author Frederic Schaffer, a political scientist at UMass Amherst, reports. Other countries requiring IDs have long lists of documents that qualify, including leases, student transcripts, medical cards, labels from prescription bottles, library cards, food subsidy cards, and public housing ID cards. And in Canada, Italy, and Portugal, if you show up without any ID, you can still vote if other voters vouch for you.

A few democracies require photo IDs—but they provide them free for all citizens. Spain, Greece, France, and Italy provide national ID cards for citizens for voting, banking, and health care. In Belgium, every citizen is automatically sent an ID card at the age of twelve.

Many states require documents to obtain an ID, such as a birth certificate, which many citizens don't have on hand. One study out of Harvard Law School found that the real cost of getting a voter ID—including obtaining paperwork, plus travel and wait time—can range from $75 to $175.

In 1966, the U.S. Supreme Court struck down a tax of $1.50 that Virginians had to pay before voting because it violated the equal protection clause of the Constitution. These voter ID costs are much higher than that.

THE VOTER FRAUD MYTH

Why do so many states require these IDs? "The ostensible justification for these stricter laws is to combat vote fraud," says political scientist Frederic Schaffer of the University of Massachusetts Amherst. "There is scant evidence, however, that the types of voter fraud which these laws prevent are a real problem."

Photo IDs can stop only one very specific kind of fraud—someone trying to impersonate a registered voter. There have been a few highly publicized cases of voter registration fraud, including a springer spaniel named Ritzy Meckler who was registered by mail as a joke. But these cases are easily caught by election officials and "there's absolutely zero evidence that anyone who has put any false information on a voter registration form has actually voted using that information," says Tova Wang, author of the book *The Politics of Voter Suppression*. How does she know? The number of successful prosecutions is "ridiculously low," she says.

Consider the work of the U.S. Justice Department: In a five-year effort to ferret out voter fraud, the department convicted fewer than a hundred people. This is in a country with more than *150 million* registered voters.

When challenged in court, states that have passed strict voter ID laws admit that voter fraud is virtually nonexistent. In Pennsylvania, the government admitted that there had been "no investigations or prosecutions of in-person voter fraud in Pennsylvania." In Indiana, "leaders concede that there has never been a case of in-person polling place impersonation in the entire history of the state." Election officials in North Carolina found that out of millions of votes cast in 2016, one, *just one,* case of voter fraud would have been prevented by the new voter ID system.

Why is voter fraud so rare? Few people are willing to face felony charges to cast just one vote. "It makes no sense for individual voters to impersonate someone," says Lorraine Minnite, a professor of public policy at Rutgers University and author of *The Myth of Voter Fraud.* "It's like committing a felony at a police station with virtually no chance of affecting the election outcome."

KNOW YOUR RIGHTS

If you show up to vote and you are told you are not registered or you don't have the required ID, take these steps:

★ Ask to sign an affidavit swearing to your eligibility.

★ Ask for a provisional ballot. Federal law entitles you to a ballot to record your vote, to be counted after your eligibility is determined.

★ If you are denied or feel intimidated, report the incident to another poll worker or local election officials, or call the Election Protection Hotline (866-OUR-VOTE) or the U.S. Department of Justice Voting Rights Hotline (800-253-3931).

HOW RARE IS VOTER FRAUD?

Between 2000 and 2010 there were:

650 MILLION VOTES CAST

47,000 UFO SIGHTINGS

441 AMERICANS KILLED BY LIGHTNING

13 CASES OF IN-PERSON VOTER IMPERSONATION

THE PEOPLE HIT HARDEST

Many members of First Nations have been hurt by voter suppression. In 2018, Native Americans in North Dakota were blindsided by a new law requiring that their ID contain a street address. Living on reservations in rural areas, many did not have street addresses. And the P.O. Boxes that they used to gather mail did not qualify. As many as seventy thousand North Dakotans—roughly 20 percent of voters—didn't have the required ID.

The elderly and people with disabilities also struggle with voting restrictions. Ten percent of citizens with disabilities—roughly 5.6 million voters—do not own a photo ID. Many elders no longer drive, and some have a hard time tracking down birth certificates from decades ago. Eighteen percent of people over the age of sixty-five—about 6 *million* citizens—lack the photo ID required in many states.

Young people also face unnecessary obstacles to voting. In 1979, the U.S. Supreme Court affirmed that college students have a right to vote in the community where they attend school. But many state ID requirements stand in students' way. For instance, Tennessee passed a law that allows faculty and staff IDs from state colleges to be used for voter identification but specifically excludes student IDs. Texas accepts permits to carry a concealed gun as proper ID to vote, but doesn't accept student IDs. Pennsylvania requires student IDs that have expiration dates, but a study found that 84 percent of students in that state attended colleges that don't include expiration dates on their student cards.

TEXAS ACCEPTS GUN PERMITS AS PROPER
VOTER ID—BUT NOT STUDENT IDS.

Transgender voters whose names have changed and people who take a married name are also at risk of being turned away at the polls. "What I used for voter registration and for identification for the last fifty-two years was not sufficient when I went to vote," says Sandra Watts, a district court judge in Texas, who had a maiden name on one form and her married name on the other. An elderly woman in Tennessee couldn't get a required photo ID card even though she presented a birth certificate, a rent receipt, and a past voter ID card because the names didn't match.

This is a challenge women could face nationwide, according to Wendy Weiser at the Brennan Center. Because many women change their last name when they get married, "a full 34 percent [of women] don't have documents proving citizenship with their current name on it," she says. That's almost 43 million women!

PART OF A RACIST SYSTEM

The racial implications of voter suppression cannot be ignored. Our nation has a history of racist voting restrictions, including property requirements, literacy tests, poll taxes, and violence and intimidation that have kept people of color from the ballot box.

Is it possible that these newer voter suppression initiatives are more of the same? Let's look at the research on whether these new requirements provide a higher barrier to voting for people of color.

People of color are disproportionately hurt by voter purges. A 2018 survey by the Public Religion Research Institute found that one in ten black and Latinx voters were incorrectly purged from voting rolls. That is twice the rate of whites (one out of twenty).

Access to polling places has historically been and continues to be restricted for people of color. In Greensboro, North Carolina, where sit-ins at a lunch counter spurred the civil rights movement in the 1960s, election officials cut the number of polling sites from sixteen to just one. Ari Berman, author of *Give Us the Ballot*, found that almost nine hundred polling places were recently closed in states with a long history of voter discrimination.

Voter ID requirements hit people of color hardest. Eight percent of voting-age white people lack a photo ID compared

NO ID, NO VOTE

Percent of people lacking IDs required in some states:

8%
White

16%
Latinx

25%
Black

Source: Brennan Center for Justice and University of California, San Diego

with 16 percent of Latinx citizens and a staggering 25 percent of black people. Researchers at the University of California, San Diego, found that strict voter ID laws disproportionately reduce turnout "of Hispanics, Blacks and mixed-race Americans in primaries and general elections."

Courts have found evidence that the disproportional impact is not coincidental. In 2016, a three-judge federal appeals court found that North Carolina's efforts to add voter ID requirements and cut early voting "target African Americans with almost surgical precision." The court had discovered that "before enacting the law, the legislature requested data on the use, by race, of a number of voting practices. Upon receipt of the race data, the General Assembly enacted legislation that restricted voting and registration in five different ways, all of which disproportionally affected African Americans."

MULTIPLE BARRIERS

Some states bundle a number of voter suppression laws together—throwing up multiple barriers to voting. North Carolina's 2013 law involved in the court case above cut early voting by a week, prohibited same-day voter registration, prohibited polling places from extending their hours due to long lines, and cut college IDs from the list of acceptable photo IDs.

The combined impact of such laws weighs heavily on our democracy, according to MIT political scientist Charles Stewart. Stewart estimates that in the November 2016 election, roughly a million people did not vote nationally because of ID or registration difficulties or long lines.

These seemingly small restrictions can affect a huge number of voters in close races, obscuring the will of the American people. "By instituting strict voter ID laws, states can alter the electorate and shift outcomes," according to research out of the University of California, San Diego.

When Wisconsin required a photo ID, roughly three hundred thousand registered voters didn't have one. In 2016, the margin of victory for presidential candidate Donald Trump in that state was only twenty-two thousand. Would these results have been different if those three hundred thousand people could have voted? In the five years leading up to 2016, Ohio purged 2 million voters from the rolls. Trump won there by half a million votes. We'll never know how the people who were blocked from voting would have voted.

Don't we want to know? Doesn't our democracy depend on it?

SMALL RESTRICTIONS CAN AFFECT A HUGE NUMBER OF VOTERS IN CLOSE RACES, OBSCURING THE WILL OF CITIZENS.

LET PEOPLE VOTE!

When Molly McGrath served as Miss Wisconsin, she traveled to more than a hundred schools across the state to encourage high school students to treasure their right to vote. But while in New York practicing law, she heard that people were being

VOTER SUPPRESSION BY THE NUMBERS

2 MILLION
Voters purged in Ohio

5.6 MILLION
Number of citizens with disabilities
who don't own a photo ID

6 MILLION
Number of people over age 65
without a current photo ID

18 MILLION
Number of Americans who do
not own state-issued photo IDs

1,000
Number of polling places
closed between 2013 and 2018

200,000
Number of Florida citizens deterred
from voting because of long lines

Sources: Brennan Center for Justice, Pew Trusts, *Stanford Law Review*, Mother Jones, *Time*, Statista.com

turned away from the polls because of Wisconsin's strict voter ID law. She returned to her home state to help people secure the documents they needed.

One morning, at a breakfast for low-income residents at a Madison church, she announced: "I'm here to make it easy for you to vote because they are passing laws to make it hard for you to vote." She drove a thirty-four-year-old man who had relocated from Chicago to get a new state ID. He brought his Illinois photo ID, his social security card, and a pay stub with his current address. The Department of Motor Vehicles demanded a birth certificate, which he did not have, and did not have the money to buy.

"I'm disappointed in my government," she says.

If you are, too, there is much you can do.

WHAT YOU CAN DO

Support Early Voting

Thirty-four states offer some early voting—but many states have cut back these opportunities. (Three states offer vote by mail, which eliminates the need for early voting.) Find out about early voting in your state at Ballotpedia's early voting page: ballotpedia.org/Early_voting.

If your state does not offer early voting or offers only limited early voting, ask your governor and state representatives to require a minimum of twenty-one days of early voting.

Ease Voter ID Restrictions

Check your state's voter ID requirement at Vote.org: www.vote
.org/voter-id-laws. If you would like to work to eliminate voter
ID laws in your state, visit the ACLU at www.aclu.org/other/
oppose-voter-id-legislation-fact-sheet.

Secure Campus Voting

Democrats and Republicans work together at some colleges
to encourage voting, including requesting polling places on
campus. At the University of Florida, students formed the
Gator Coalition for Civic Engagement and organized rides
to get students to the polls. Vassar College political groups
formed the nonpartisan REV Up to encourage voting, offer
rides, and distribute candidate information. To improve
access to voting at your college, visit the Campus Vote Project at campusvoteproject.org/students and Students Learn
Students Vote at www.studentslearnstudentsvote.org/the
-checklist.

Help Voters

VoteRiders offers citizens financial and legal help to people
having trouble securing a required ID. Sign up to volunteer at
www.voteriders.org/get-involved.

Sign up at Carpool Vote to give rides to the polls to people
lacking transportation: actionnetwork.org/forms/i-can-offer
-a-ride-to-the-polls?source=twitter&.

Repeated investigations show there is virtually no in-person voter fraud nationally.

—U.S. Circuit Court judge and Republican legal scholar Richard Posner

Voters shouldn't lose their right to vote simply because they vote infrequently.

—Ohio Democratic Party chair David Pepper

Republicans should be less afraid of how people vote and more concerned with making sure they do vote.

—Michael Steele, former chair of the Republican National Committee

We have to demand attention. What the states with the highest voter suppression have in common is that they also have the highest rates of poverty.

—Rev. William Barber II, leader of Moral Mondays

Would you believe that *millions* of American citizens have no representation in the federal government? Many of these citizens serve in the military and pay taxes, but can't vote for president and have no power in Congress. They are not felons or underage or otherwise blocked from voting power. They simply live in areas that are not allowed to become states.

From the time Washington, D.C., became our nation's capital, it has been controlled by the federal government rather than a state government. Because the District of Columbia is not a state, the seven hundred thousand citizens who live there are not allowed to govern themselves nor enjoy representation in the Congress they host. D.C. residents pay the second-highest federal taxes per person in the country, adding up to more than *$3 billion* in federal taxes. That's a lot of taxation without representation. More than two hundred thousand men and women from the District of Columbia have served in the U.S. military. Roughly two thousand D.C. citizens have given their lives for our country. And yet they don't have access to the same voting rights as other Americans.

Puerto Rico, claimed as a territory at the end of the Spanish-American War in 1898, is home to 3.5 million U.S. citizens. That's a larger population than more than twenty states already in our union. Puerto Ricans living on the island don't pay federal income tax, but they do make full tax contributions to social security and Medicare.

Because they are not states, Washington, D.C., and Puerto Rico lack congressional representation with full voting powers. We amended the Constitution in 1961 to allow D.C. residents to vote for electors in presidential races. Puerto Ricans aren't allowed to vote for president, except in primaries held by political parties.

But it's more than just representation these territories seek. "We want to be treated like any other state," says nonvoting D.C. House delegate Eleanor Norton. "To understand statehood, you have to understand what it means to be unequal in your own country."

Statehood comes with not only voting power, but often support from the federal government. A recent estimate puts Puerto Rico in line for roughly $2 billion to $5.5 billion more federal funding a year if it were to become a state. Investment in infrastructure and education can spur growth and economic development that can help new states rise out of poverty. Since our founding, we've added thirty-seven states to our country. The most recent were Hawaii and Alaska in 1959. Both improved economically after joining the union.

Part of the problem is that there is no official process to become a state. Historically, Congress has applied the following procedure: The state petitions Congress for statehood, Congress passes a joint resolution accepting the territory as a state, and the president signs it.

Residents of D.C. are clear in their support of statehood. In 2016, 86 percent voted to petition Congress to become a state. They've taken other steps too. When Alaska pushed for statehood in 1956, it sent a "shadow" delegation to Congress demanding to be recognized as voting members. Since 1990, the District of Columbia has been sending two shadow senators and a shadow representative to Congress. These unpaid elected officials are not allowed to vote. Instead, they try to educate their colleagues about the plight of their citizens. The advocates have also introduced a statehood bill into Congress, which now has more than 130 cosponsors. But without a national outcry in support of their efforts, the bill faces widespread indifference from the rest of Congress.

In 2017, 97 percent of voting Puerto Ricans supported statehood. That sounds overwhelming, but many people boycotted the election and only a quarter of registered citizens voted. (Some Puerto Ricans want to remain separate to protect their culture or to avoid the burden of federal income taxes.) But a survey of survivors of Hurricane Maria by the Kaiser Family Foundation and the *Washington Post* suggests support for statehood is growing. Almost half said they want Puerto Rico to become a state, 26 percent would rather it remain a territory, and 10 percent want full independence.

Like D.C., Puerto Rico has tried to move statehood forward. In 2018, Puerto Rico introduced a Statehood Commission with a shadow delegation. Former governor Ricardo Rosselló appointed two shadow senators and five shadow House members to Congress, the number they would be allocated if they achieved statehood. This commission works to make the case to Congress for admitting Puerto Rico into the union. The former governor also wrote a formal letter to President Donald

Trump requesting statehood. And Puerto Rico's resident commissioner—the island's only official representative in Congress who has a voice but no vote—Jenniffer González-Colón, introduced a bill in Congress to achieve statehood by 2021. The bill has more than fifty cosponsors. "I'm pleased to be one of the sponsors," said Rep. Rob Bishop (R-Utah). "I look forward to the day 51 is a reality." But the bill has never been put to a vote.

Part of the lack of movement is that the measure would need widespread support, yet almost half of Americans don't even realize Puerto Ricans are American citizens. Another obstacle is that a busy Congress has little incentive to find time to address the issue. "[Congress] will just put off a decision for further down the road," says Carlos Vargas-Ramos, a research associate at the Hunter College Center for Puerto Rican Studies. "I don't see major forces operating to change the status of Puerto Rico in the short term."

THE 52-STATE FLAG

PUERTO RICO FLAG

D.C. FLAG

The United States has other territories without voting rights—Guam, the U.S. Virgin Islands, American Samoa, and the Northern Mariana Islands—but Puerto Rico is the only one with such a large population that has requested statehood to no avail.

ALMOST HALF OF AMERICANS DON'T EVEN REALIZE PUERTO RICANS ARE AMERICAN CITIZENS.

Still, many Americans are supportive. Nearly half favor statehood efforts and just a third are opposed. Support is not limited by party. Both Democrats and Republicans have expressed support for statehood at their party conventions. Former Democratic president Barack Obama supports statehood for both D.C. and Puerto Rico. The D.C. Republican Party backs D.C. statehood and the national Republican Party includes Puerto Rican statehood in its platform, stating: "We support the right of the United States citizens of Puerto Rico to be admitted to the Union as a fully sovereign state if they freely so determine." Senator Bernie Sanders (I) thinks it is "morally wrong for American citizens who pay federal taxes, fight in our wars, and live in our country to be denied the basic right to full congressional representation."

While being awarded statehood can take decades, no request from a U.S. territory has ever been refused. So why delay? Millions of citizens in Washington, D.C., and Puerto Rico are ready to be fully welcomed into the United States of America.

WHAT YOU CAN DO

Learn how to support D.C. statehood, including signing a petition, at statehood.dc.gov.

Join a student Street Team to educate people about D.C. statehood at www.dcvote.org/civic-engagement.

To learn more about Puerto Rico's statehood efforts, sign a petition, or lobby your members of Congress, visit www.pr51st.com.

DO THEY DESERVE STATEHOOD?

D.C. FACTS

US Citizens!

Population larger than two states

Pays MORE federal taxes than 20 states

86% of DC voted for DC statehood in 2016

PUERTO RICO FACTS

US Citizens!

Population larger than 21 states

Paid $3.5 BILLION in Federal Taxes in 2016

97% of PR voted for statehood in 2017

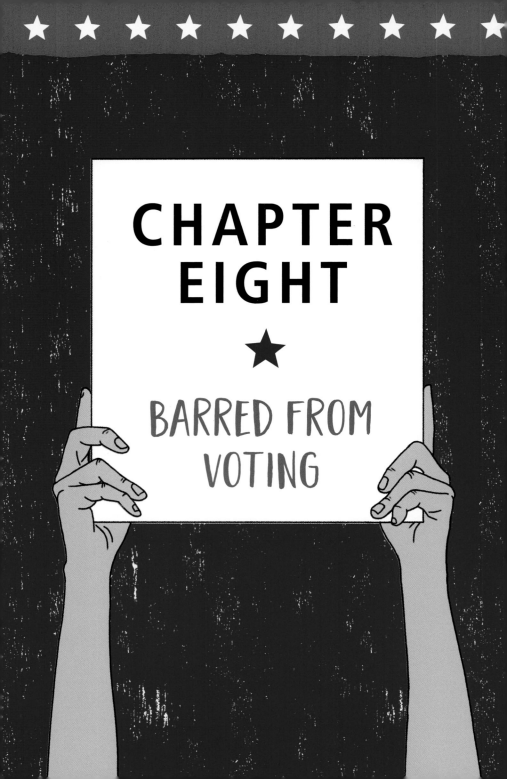

MORE THAN *4 MILLION* AMERICANS CANNOT VOTE BECAUSE OF A FELONY CONVICTION—3.3 MILLION ARE NOT EVEN IN PRISON ANYMORE.

As a young man, Desmond Meade became addicted to drugs and served three years in prison for felony gun possession. Once paroled, he found himself homeless, unemployed, and still addicted. One day, standing by a railroad track, he considered throwing himself under a train. But the train never came.

So Meade crossed the tracks and entered rehab. He lived in a homeless shelter and attended a local college. He graduated from the paralegal program, got a bachelor's degree, and went on to obtain a law degree from the Florida International Law

School. He's now married, has five children, and leads a non-profit organization.

But when his wife ran for a seat in the Florida House of Representatives, Meade could not vote for her. In Florida at the time, a felony conviction meant a lifetime ban from voting. "I paid my debt to society and served my time," says Meade, the executive director of the Florida Rights Restoration Coalition. "Now I should have the opportunity to have my voice heard."

THIRTY-THREE STATES BAR CITIZENS FROM VOTING ON THE BASIS OF A PAST CONVICTION.

Barring felons from voting might seem like common sense—why would we want criminals voting? The reality is that more than *4 million* citizens are disenfranchised, or denied the right to vote. More than *3 million* of these people are out of prison and are still barred from the ballot box. "To be shut out of the democratic process is like a perpetual punishment and slap in the face, saying you're never going to be a citizen," says Meade.

SHOULD YOUR RIGHT TO VOTE DEPEND ON WHERE YOU LIVE?

There is no federal law banning felons from voting; whether felons or ex-felons can cast a ballot varies dramatically by state. That's because the United States operates like fifty-one different countries when it comes to what counts as a felony

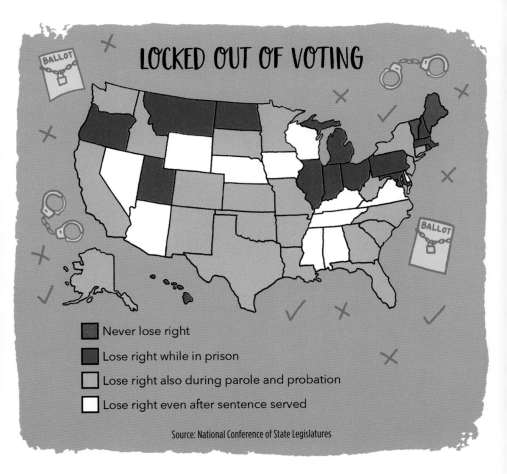

LOCKED OUT OF VOTING

Never lose right

Lose right while in prison

Lose right also during parole and probation

Lose right even after sentence served

Source: National Conference of State Legislatures

and felon voting laws. Two states—Maine and Vermont— never revoke voting rights. Fourteen states and the District of Columbia restrict the right only while people are in prison.

But many bar voting for what seem like minor offenses, such as possessing less than an ounce of marijuana, driving with a suspended license, or catching a lobster whose tail is too short. In Mississippi, if you pay $100 for something with a bad check, you can lose your voting rights *forever.* Mississippi permanently bars voting for twenty-one different crimes, including bad check writing, bribery, and shoplifting.

SERVING TIME

Prison: A facility run by the state or federal government where people convicted of crimes are held for punishment and to keep the public safe.

Jail: Similar to prison but run by local governments, often with lower security and more rehabilitation programs. For sentences of less than a year, felons sometimes serve their time in jail. Jails also house people awaiting trial.

Probation: An alternative sentence to imprisonment. During probation, convicts are supervised and expected to follow specific conditions, such as getting permission to travel, taking drug or alcohol tests, or holding down a job.

Parole: Early release from prison, before the full sentence is served, with similar conditions to probation.

Two states—Kentucky and Iowa—take away voting rights for *all felons* for essentially their *entire lives.* No vote for felons in prison. No vote for people who were convicted but *not* sentenced to prison, only to probation. No vote for people released from prison on parole. No vote for people who completed their time in prison, their time on probation, or their time on parole. No vote for people who have served their entire sentence and have reintegrated into the community—even after decades. Until 2018, Florida took the same approach.

In these restrictive states, getting the vote back requires a long, complicated, and often expensive path. In Florida from 2007 until 2018, after completing felony sentences, people had to wait five to seven years to submit an application and supporting documents to get voting rights restored. Then it took an average of *nine more years* to get a hearing from the clemency board, which met only four times a year.

The time and complexity of the process kept most people from trying. Still, many citizens who reentered society cared deeply about their right to vote. More than one hundred thousand Floridians applied each year. Not that it did much good—only about four hundred got their rights back annually. The result was that a staggering 1.7 million Floridians *who had completed their sentences* continued to be barred from voting.

THE UNITED STATES HAS LESS THAN 5 PERCENT OF THE WORLD'S POPULATION BUT ALMOST A *QUARTER* OF THE WORLD'S PRISON POPULATION.

WHAT IN THE WORLD?

One reason so many Americans are affected by felon disenfranchisement is that the United States puts so many people in prison. We have less than 5 percent of the world's population but almost *a quarter* of the world's prison population. In fact, we have the highest incarceration rate in the world.

Also, no other democracy in the world strips citizens of their right to vote for their entire lives for committing a crime. Twenty-one countries, including Austria, Canada, Denmark, Spain, and Switzerland, do not restrict voting, even for prisoners. In twenty-six European nations, voting may be limited for those serving long sentences or for prisoners convicted of specific crimes against the state or democratic order. Almost all of these restore voting rights upon release. In these criminal justice systems, if you make a mistake and break the law, you are punished. After you pay your debt, you return fully to society.

HOW BAD IS A FELONY?

Most felons who are barred from voting in the United States have completed their sentences and live in our communities. Roughly 3.3 million ex-felons live among us, work, pay taxes, volunteer, and raise families in our neighborhoods—but can't vote.

It's easy to hear the word *felon* and assume it refers to bank robbers and murderers. But the vast majority of felons have been convicted of nonviolent crimes (82 percent), mainly

THE UNITED STATES LOCKS UP THE MOST PEOPLE

Incarceration rates per 100,000 people

United States	670
Rwanda	434
Russia	413
Brazil	325
Australia	167
Spain	126
China	118
Canada	114
France	102
Austria	94
Germany	78
Denmark	59
Sweden	57
India	33

Source: The Sentencing Project

HAVE YOU COMMITTED A FELONY?

Here is short list of common activities and the felony charges they could bring you:

★ Taking a fake sick day from work—Scheme or artifice to defraud the company

★ Telling a park ranger you cleaned your campsite when you did not—Making false statements to a federal official

★ Illegally downloading a movie or song without payment—Copyright infringement

★ Using someone else's Wi-Fi without permission—Unlawful access to computers and networks

★ Making changes to your friend's Facebook page as a joke—Wire fraud

★ Failing to report tips—Tax evasion

★ Egging a mailbox—Vandalism of federal property

★ Violating a website's terms of use—Computer fraud and abuse

crimes related to drugs. In fact, half of federal prison inmates are there for drug offenses.

You might be surprised to learn that it is quite possible—even probable—that you have committed or will commit a felony sometime in your life. Even the most upstanding citizens "cannot predict with any reasonable assurance whether a wide range of seemingly ordinary activities might be regarded by federal prosecutors as felonies," writes attorney Harvey Silver-glate in his book *Three Felonies a Day.*

People are often surprised to be charged and convicted of a felony—and can be even more surprised when they learn that they have lost their right to vote. Forever.

AFRAID TO VOTE

Crystal Mason, a Texan, did not know that being on probation for tax fraud barred her from voting. When Mason went to vote, a poll worker who couldn't find her name on the rolls helped her fill out a provisional ballot. That mistake put Mason in prison—with a five-year sentence.

Keith Sellers of North Carolina was pulled over for running a red light while heading home after dinner out with his daughters. He ended up in handcuffs, his daughters crying in the back seat. He was charged with illegal voting—he also voted while on probation. Conviction comes with a sentence of up to two years. Not one person—neither the judge, the lawyers, nor his probation officer—warned him that he had lost the right to vote. "I thought I was practicing my right," he says.

In 2017, only eleven people were convicted of illegal voting, according to the Heritage Foundation. Out of the millions of votes cast, that's a tiny number. But it's a big deal to the people convicted—and to other ex-offenders unsure of their right to vote.

Because of the threat of steep penalties, many ex-prisoners are afraid to vote. They hear through the grapevine that they

WILL DO TIME IN PRISON

ALL MEN — 1 in 9

LATINX MEN — 1 in 5

BLACK MEN — 1 in 3

Source: The Sentencing Project

lost their right, so they don't register when they're eligible. Even people convicted of lesser crimes called misdemeanors often believe they can't vote.

When the downsides of voting illegally are so harsh, relative to the benefit, many ex-offenders won't take the risk of voting even if they think they may be eligible, says Marc Meredith, associate professor of political science at the University of Pennsylvania.

Making it even more confusing is that the right to vote has been given and taken away by governors and court rulings. Imagine you committed a felony and lost your right to vote. While on parole you hear that parolees now have the right to vote. So you register. But before you have the chance to vote, you hear that the new governor reversed the executive order.

Someone assures you that the new policy won't affect anyone who is already registered. Now imagine that you could get thrown back in prison as a repeat offender for getting it wrong.

Would you risk that possibility just to vote?

BARRED WHILE BLACK

The loss of voting rights because of a felony conviction hits people of color hardest, especially black people. Nationally, one in thirteen black Americans have been stripped of their vote because of a felony conviction. It's *one in five* in Kentucky, Tennessee, and Virginia. Compare this to one in fifty of the non-black population.

Something is going on, and it's not that black people commit more crimes. A big problem is drug laws, which tend to be unevenly and racially enforced. A black person is more likely to be arrested, convicted, and face a stiffer sentence than a white person *for the same drug-related crime*. Black and white people use drugs at the same rate and yet blacks are almost four times more likely to be arrested for drugs than whites. And most of these arrests—four in five—are for possession, not selling. Once convicted, black people get longer sentences—10 percent longer.

A DARK HISTORY

What would you think about barring felons from voting if you learned that the policy was an effort to stop black people and poor people from voting? History suggests this is the case.

After the Civil War and the end of slavery, many Southern states enacted laws to take the vote away from African Americans to weaken the political strength of the newly freed population. In Virginia, felon voting restrictions were ramped up in 1902 along with poll taxes and literacy tests, all designed to keep blacks from voting. A Virginia state senator said the provisions would "eliminate the [racial slur] as a political factor in this State in less than five years, so that in no single county of the Commonwealth will there be the least concern felt for the complete supremacy of the white race in the affairs of government."

Several Southern states targeted offenses they thought were more likely to be committed by poor or black people, such as property crimes. In Mississippi, politicians called for disenfranchisement for burglary, theft, and arson, but not murder. As a result, you could lose your vote in Mississippi for stealing a cow but not for killing the farmer. Likewise, in Alabama, someone would be disenfranchised for beating his wife, but not for killing her.

Whether this is the intention now, taking the vote away from offenders and ex-offenders still keeps many black people from voting. But people of all races have been swept up in the mess. "The original intent was to keep freed slaves from voting," says Desmond Meade, "but this policy has managed to transcend racial lines and now impacts more non-African Americans than African Americans. . . . This impacts so many families."

NO CONVICTION AND NO VOTE

The problem hits even before a conviction. No one is supposed to lose the right to vote when arrested. Our court system, with its presumption of innocence, protects against that. But in practice, more than four hundred thousand people do lose their right to vote because of arrest. While held in jail or prison while awaiting trial, they are technically eligible to vote but have no access to voting. They can't leave to cast their vote in a polling place and there is no process for them to get an absentee ballot.

COMMUNITIES SUFFER

What happens in neighborhoods where chunks of the population are not allowed to vote? The government loses vital information about what people in those communities need. Offenders and ex-offenders might have valuable insights to share, including ideas about the criminal justice system, the way prisons are run, and public safety. Why should those views be ignored?

Politicians tend to overlook whole neighborhoods when many people in that neighborhood can't vote. Studies show that candidates are less likely to campaign in neighborhoods where many ex-offenders live—and less government spending flows into them.

Lacking a voice can breed apathy. If you believe no one is listening, why would you care about the political process and

BARRED FROM VOTING BY THE NUMBERS

NUMBER OF AMERICANS BARRED FROM
VOTING WHILE IN JAIL:

72,200

NUMBER OF AMERICANS BARRED FROM
VOTING WHILE ON PAROLE:

504,100

NUMBER OF AMERICANS BARRED FROM
VOTING WHILE IN PRISON:

1.3 MILLION

NUMBER OF AMERICANS BARRED FROM
VOTING *AFTER* COMPLETING SENTENCE:

3.1 MILLION

Source: The Sentencing Project, 2016

voting? Apathy can spread. Voting tends to be a community endeavor. If people who have served their sentences can't vote, they are less likely to talk with their family, friends, and neighbors about voting.

Children also lose opportunities to see citizenship in action. "I'd like to set a good example for my children, grandchildren, nieces, and nephews to take an active role in voting," says ex-offender David Waller.

VOTING PROMOTES PUBLIC SAFETY

Voting encourages participation in public life and strengthens ties with the community. Research suggests voters are more likely to volunteer, reach out to elected officials, and keep abreast of local issues. Permitting voting is a simple, inexpensive way to offer ex-offenders a chance to rethink who they are in the community. Voting actually *lowers* the chance that someone released from prison will reoffend. In one study, ex-offenders who could vote were rearrested half as often as nonvoters. Researchers surmised that "voting appears to be part of a package of pro-social behavior that is linked to desistance from crime."

That's why so many law enforcement organizations support ex-felon voting. Officers who supervise felons in jails and prisons advocate for restoration of voting rights after all sentences have been served. In its policy statement, the American Correctional Association "affirms that voting is a fundamental right in a democracy and it considers a ban on voting after a felon is discharged from correctional supervision to be contradictory to the goals of a democracy, the rehabilitation of felons, and their successful reentry to the community."

The American Probation and Parole Association, a group of officers who work with people serving sentences out in the community, takes it even further, advocating for full voting rights for all people who are not imprisoned.

Most Americans agree. Eight in ten surveyed support voting rights for all those who have completed their sentences. Nearly two-thirds would extend the right to people on probation or parole.

What would happen if laws were changed to reflect what most Americans want? Roughly 3.3 million more citizens would be able to share their views on candidates, ballot measures, and important issues that affect their lives, such as education, health care, criminal justice reform, and the economy.

EIGHT IN TEN AMERICANS SUPPORT VOTING RIGHTS FOR ALL EX-OFFENDERS WHO HAVE SERVED THEIR TIME.

WHAT PROBATION AND PAROLE OFFICERS WANT

"WHEREAS, the loss of the right to vote is not based on a need to protect the integrity of the electoral process and the justice system; and

WHEREAS, disenfranchisement of felons is disproportionately affecting an increasingly large segment of the population and their families; and

WHEREAS, disenfranchisement laws work against the successful reentry of offenders;

THEREFORE, BE IT RESOLVED that the American Probation and Parole Association advocates the restoration of voting rights upon completion of an offender's prison sentence and advocates no loss of voting rights while on community supervision."

A CONSTITUTIONAL RIGHT TO VOTE?

"Nowhere in the U.S. Constitution does it say that my right can ever be taken away from me," says ex-offender Alonzo Malone Jr. "I've read it and read it, and I'm not illiterate. I feel cheated and robbed."

The Fifteenth Amendment to the Constitution states: "The right of citizens of the United States to vote shall not be denied or abridged by the United States or by any State on account of race, color, or previous condition of servitude."

Some Americans support an amendment to the Constitution or an act of Congress to make the right to vote crystal clear. The law might read: "Every citizen of the United States, who is of legal voting age, shall have the fundamental right to vote in any public election held in the jurisdiction in which the citizen resides."

Guaranteeing the right to vote would separate our democracy from the criminal justice system. A person's right to vote would not depend on local, regional, or state differences in criminal or voting laws. It would not depend on whether a judge is strict or lenient, favors prison or parole, or acts with racial or class bias. Instead we'd have universal suffrage, in which all Americans have equal access and equal opportunity to share their political choices.

FREE THE VOTE

If all Americans had the right to vote, jails and prisons across the country would have a process for people to exercise that right. It would completely alleviate the confusion for election officials and the public about who is eligible to vote—and stop making citizens afraid to vote.

Such a change is not as radical as it might seem. In fact, it's already happening. Vermont and Maine do not tie voting rights to the criminal justice system. And prisoners in Puerto Rico, a U.S. territory, can vote in Democratic and Republican presidential primaries. In all three places, voting has gone smoothly. In Vermont, for instance, prison staff alert inmates to their right to vote three months before an election. The prison library offers information on how to register and request an absentee ballot. Then prisoners vote and mail in their ballots. "The last thing we want to do is start putting up insurmountable barriers to participation in civic life because someone may have been convicted of a crime," said Republican Party spokesperson Mike Donahue. "People's right to vote is sacred."

Prisoners have plenty of time to research the issues and their candidates. "I look at it like, OK, it could affect my family, could affect people I care about," says Maine prisoner Doug Burr. "So I show interest in it, I get involved. I read a lot. I watch the news so I try to stay up, as much as possible, anyways."

RESTORE THE VOTE, RESTORE DEMOCRACY

Efforts are already afoot at the national level to fix the patchwork of voting laws. Members of Congress have introduced the Democracy Restoration Act, which would restore the vote in federal elections to the 3.3 million citizens who have been released from prison. The bill now has more than thirty cosponsors in the House and more than twenty in the Senate.

DEMOCRACY RESTORATION ACT

"The right of an individual who is a citizen of the United States to vote in any election for federal office shall not be denied or abridged because that individual has been convicted of a criminal offense unless such individual is serving a felony sentence in a correctional institution or facility at the time of the election."

Statewide efforts are also moving apace. After the 2016 election, Alabama shortened the list of crimes that stripped people of voting rights. A New York governor gave an order to restore voting to people on parole and a Virginia governor restored rights to more than 170,000 people.

Courts have been involved, too. A federal judge called the Florida system "crushingly restrictive" and ruled that it violated the First Amendment right to freedom of speech and the Fourteenth Amendment right to due process. But the case got bogged down in appeals.

Florida citizens didn't wait for the courts to fix the problem. More than 750,000 people signed a petition supporting an amendment to the state constitution. In 2018, the state voted on Amendment 4 to restore voting rights to about 1.4 million Floridians who had served their time, excluding only people convicted of specific offenses such as murder and sexual assault. The constitutional amendment required 60 percent of the votes to pass.

In November 2018, 64 percent of Florida voters approved the measure, in what many consider to be one of the most significant expansions of voting rights in the state's history.

As soon as he could, Desmond Meade, president of the Florida Rights Restoration Coalition, registered to vote along with other ex-felons, whom he calls "returning citizens." "There were a lot of tears of joy that were shed. Some of the [election officials] were crying," says Meade. "It was just a very emotional day. We were celebrating the expansion of democracy."

TO THE POLLS

Volunteers in Florida and other places around the country are working to get the word out to ex-offenders who are eligible to vote. Even people who have left prison have gotten involved. After serving three months behind bars, Steve Huerta began knocking on doors in Texas to encourage ex-felons to register and vote. To him, voting is the key to turning around lives—and neighborhoods. "This is an entirely new voting bloc," he says. "It's a political game changer for struggling communities."

To many, the right to vote is precious. Ex-offender Deirdre Wilson describes her return to voting this way: "As I ran my pen back and forth over the small space for the candidates I chose to vote for, I felt responsible and powerful," she says. "Responsible as a member of our society and powerful to have a say in the process."

WHAT YOU CAN DO

For a quick check to see if felons and ex-felons can vote in your state and under what circumstances, visit www.sentencing project.org/publications/felony-disenfranchisement-a-primer.

If you have been convicted of a felony and you need more detailed information, check campaignlegal.org/restoreyourvote.

To join statewide efforts to restore the vote to returning citizens or to help register them, visit the Sentencing Project at www.sentencingproject.org/state-contacts.

Contact your governor and state representatives and ask them to restore voting rights to felons and ex-felons. Type in your zip code to Who Represents Me? to get their contact information: www.270towin.com/elected-officials.

Create a petition and gather signatures online here: www.change.org/start-a-petition.

Write letters to the editors of your local and statewide newspapers. (For your newspaper's address and submission process, type "Letters to the Editor" and the name of your newspaper into your internet browser.)

Find out if your U.S. senator or representative is a cosponsor of the Democracy Restoration Act and if not, ask them to sign on. Refer to www.brennancenter.org/legislation/democracy-restoration-act for information on the bill and cosponsors. You can also search www.congress.gov by bill number or name. (Please note that the name of the bill and the number can change over different congressional sessions.)

The right to vote is a sacred one. I'm pushing for restoring voting rights at the state level, and I also will push for changes at the federal level.

—U.S. SENATOR RAND PAUL (R-KY.)

People have served their time and done their probation, I want you back in society. I want you feeling good about yourself. I want you voting, getting a job, paying taxes.

—GOV. TERRY MCAULIFFE (D-VA.), WHO RETURNED THE VOTE TO ROUGHLY TWO HUNDRED THOUSAND PEOPLE

I was asked . . . about felon disenfranchisement in our state. I was in favor of fixing the process. Because these men and women have paid their debt to society. Because limiting the rights of others undermines our democracy. Because it's morally right.

—CHARLIE CRIST (R-FLA.), WHO RESTORED VOTING RIGHTS TO MORE THAN ONE HUNDRED THOUSAND EX-OFFENDERS WHILE SERVING AS GOVERNOR OF FLORIDA

The United States may have the most restrictive disenfranchisement policy in the world. Such prohibitions on the right to vote undermine both the voting system and the fundamental rights of ex-offenders.

—U.S. REP. JOHN CONYERS JR. (D-MICH.), WHO INTRODUCED THE DEMOCRACY RESTORATION ACT INTO CONGRESS IN 2015

YOUTH VOTE

EIGHT MILLION U.S. CITIZENS WHO CAN HOLD JOBS, GET MARRIED, PAY TAXES, AND DRIVE ON PUBLIC ROADS ARE NOT ALLOWED TO VOTE.

On Election Day in November 2013, Takoma Park, Maryland, made history. It became the first city in the United States to lower the voting age for local elections to sixteen.

Blair High School junior Ben Miller, who worked part-time at a gelato store and played in a rock band, was the first voter under eighteen to register.

Alanna Natanson became the first person in the United States under age eighteen to cast a ballot. "I think it's important that we all do our part to show our government that we care," she says. "We want our government to represent us."

In 2015, young people in Greenbelt, Maryland, took up the idea. When citizens there were first asked if they supported lowering the voting age for city elections from eighteen to sixteen, a whopping 77 percent opposed it. Over the next couple of years, teens created videos describing their involvement in the community and what voting would mean to them. They attended rallies for City Council members and brought the issue up in meetings and debates. They testified on local issues that mattered to them. They submitted letters to the editor of local newspapers. They created brochures and knocked on doors.

When talking to the public, seventeen-year-old Julia Sharapi of Greenbelt's Youth Advisory Committee got some pushback. People told her: "You are alright, but my grandkids are irresponsible." But she didn't give up. "It's hard when you're told that people our age are disrespectful and irresponsible, but we kept moving forward," she says.

Ema Smith, also seventeen at the time, faced the same resistance at first. "If you explain the reasoning behind lowering the age, people will often change their minds," she says.

And they did. In 2017, 54 percent of voters supported the effort—and it passed.

> "IF YOU EXPLAIN THE REASONING BEHIND LOWERING THE AGE, PEOPLE WILL OFTEN CHANGE THEIR MINDS."

Currently there are 8 million citizens ages sixteen and seventeen in the United States. These younger citizens can hold jobs, get married, pay taxes, and operate dangerous machines—cars—on public roads. But they have almost no say in electing the people who will make decisions that influence all aspects of their lives, including the quality and safety of their high schools and colleges, their health care options and tax burden, and the wars they may one day be called on to fight.

What would our democracy look like if they were granted the vote?

Sixteen- and seventeen-year-olds are already voting in three cities in Maryland and one in California. Efforts have been afoot in Fairfax, Richmond, Fresno, Sacramento, and San Francisco, California; Broward County, Florida; Shelburne and Ashfield, Massachusetts; Bridgeton, New Jersey; and in Washington, D.C., Illinois, Colorado, New York, and Texas. In fact, attempts to lower the voting age to sixteen have been launched in almost half of the states.

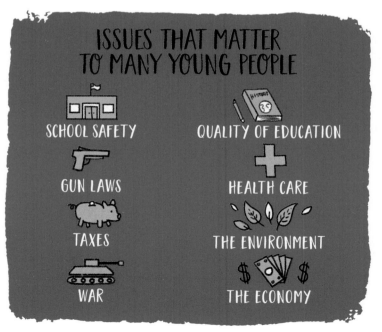

ISSUES THAT MATTER
TO MANY YOUNG PEOPLE

SCHOOL SAFETY

GUN LAWS

TAXES

WAR

QUALITY OF EDUCATION

HEALTH CARE

THE ENVIRONMENT

THE ECONOMY

LOWERING THE VOTING AGE IN THE U.S.

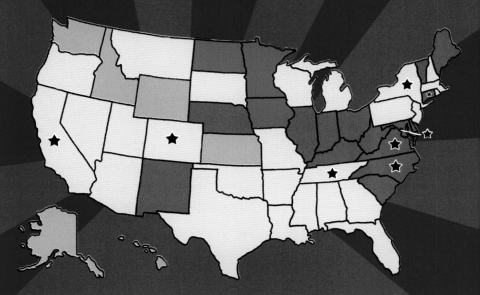

17-YEAR-OLDS WHO WILL BE 18 ON ELECTION DAY:

 Can vote in primary elections

 Can vote in Democratic and Republican caucuses

 Can vote in the Democratic caucuses

 Cannot vote in primaries

★ States where some 16-year-olds can vote or with campaigns to lower the voting age

AND AROUND THE WORLD

OTHER COUNTRIES THAT HAVE A VOTING AGE UNDER 18

AGE 16

Argentina

Austria

Bosnia and Herzegovina
(if employed)

Brazil

Croatia
(if employed)

Cuba

Dominican Republic
(if married)

Ecuador

Estonia
(local elections only)

Germany
(seven out of sixteen states
have lowered the voting age to
16 for local elections only)

Guernsey

Hungary
(if married)

Indonesia
(if married)

Isle of Man

Jersey

Malta
(local elections only)

Nicaragua

Scotland
(in non-federal
elections only)

Serbia
(if employed)

Slovenia
(if employed)

★ ★ ★ ★ ★ ★ ★ ★ ★ ★ ★

AGE 17

Greece

Indonesia

Israel
(local elections only)

North Korea

Sudan

Seychelles

Switzerland
(in the state of Glarus for
regional elections only)

Source: National Youth Rights Association

IS IT CONSTITUTIONAL?

The right to vote in the United States was first granted only to white men who owned land. Over time it was expanded to include people who don't own land, indigenous peoples, black people, and women. The voting age, determined by states, had historically been twenty-one.

Then in 1971, the U.S. Congress passed the Twenty-Sixth Amendment to the Constitution, lowering the voting age from twenty-one to eighteen. The main impetus was the Vietnam War. People objected to the country drafting eighteen-year-olds to fight without allowing them to vote. The Twenty-Sixth Amendment was so popular and had such overwhelming bipartisan support that it was the fastest amendment to be ratified by the states. It extended the vote to 11 million young adults.

The amendment makes it unconstitutional to block anyone eighteen years or older from voting because of their age. But it leaves open the possibility of adjusting the voting age downward. Lowering the voting age, even in national elections, "is constitutional," says Nathaniel Persily, a professor of law at Stanford University. "The amendment prevents against discrimination, it doesn't prevent against greater inclusion."

DO TEENS DESERVE A SAY?

Teenagers hold down jobs, run businesses, juggle education while supporting families, and contribute to the community in record numbers. Teens' civic engagement is impressive. Almost 16 million young people volunteer in the community—with high schoolers the most likely of all age populations to volunteer.

WHAT IN THE WORLD?

The United States would not be the first nation to make this change. In parts of Europe and South America, the voting age has already been dropped. The effort to lower the voting age to sixteen in Austria in 2007 was so popular that political parties argued over whose idea it was! When citizens of Scotland were voting on independence, people sixteen and older were allowed to vote—and young people did so in great numbers. Sixteen countries, including Argentina, Austria, Brazil, Ecuador, Serbia, and Switzerland, all allow voting in some or all elections for people ages sixteen and up. So why not sixteen- and seventeen-year-olds in this country?

Many teens play adult roles in their families. For instance, millions of young people in immigrant families act as translators for first-generation parents who speak little or no English. Almost a million and a half young people are responsible for caring for sick family members, feeding them, administering medication, and accompanying them to doctors' appointments and therapy. On any given day, 30 percent of teens who have younger siblings are responsible for them.

Many support themselves and their families financially. Roughly 2 million sixteen- and seventeen-year-olds held down jobs in 2017, according to the Bureau of Labor Statistics. One-third of working youth contribute more than 20 percent to the total income of their households, according to the American Community Survey. One out of every ten working youth is

TEENS HAVE ALREADY GROWN UP

Number of teens who volunteer in their community

61 MILLION

Number of teens who hold down jobs

2 MILLION

Number of teens who provide essential health care to family member

1.5 MILLION

Amount teens under the age of 18 pay in taxes every year

$700 MILLION

Percent of working youth who contribute more than 20% of their family's total income

A THIRD

Percent of working youth responsible for **MORE THAN HALF** of their family's income

ONE IN TEN

responsible for more than half of their household's income.

People under eighteen pay taxes, too, to the tune of $700 million a year. Without the vote, this is taxation without representation, one of the core reasons our nation declared independence from Great Britain.

One of the great features of democracy is that politicians have to be responsive to people who have a say at the polls. "From a public official's point of view," says Kate Stewart, who was elected mayor after Takoma Park lowered the voting age, "it makes you pay attention a lot more to issues that are important to 16- and 17-year-olds."

OLD ENOUGH FOR JAIL

People under eighteen have to follow adult laws and often face adult consequences when they violate the law. A quarter million people under age eighteen are tried, sentenced, and jailed as adults every year. Does it make sense that we consider sixteen- and seventeen-year-olds as mature adults, responsible for their own actions, when they commit a crime, while also insisting that they are not mature, adult, or responsible enough to vote?

ARE YOUNG PEOPLE COMPETENT TO VOTE?

One argument against lowering the voting age is that sixteen- and seventeen-year-olds aren't competent to make informed choices during an election. Research contradicts this claim.

Recent advances in brain and developmental research have uncovered interesting differences between two kinds of decision-making. Decision-making when emotional, tired, in a group, under pressure from others, or in a hurry is called "hot" cognition. Decision-making in a calm situation when there is ample time to think and consider the facts is considered "cold" cognition.

Laurence Steinberg, professor of psychology at Temple University and one of the world's leading experts on adolescence, notes that while it may be true that sixteen-year-olds are not at their best making decisions when tired, stressed, or in a group of other teens ("hot" cognition), sixteen-year-old brains are fully developed to handle calm, reasoned decision-making. Sixteen-year-olds have as much capacity as adults to gather and consider facts and information, weigh pros and cons, and logically analyze ideas and situations when they have enough time, he says.

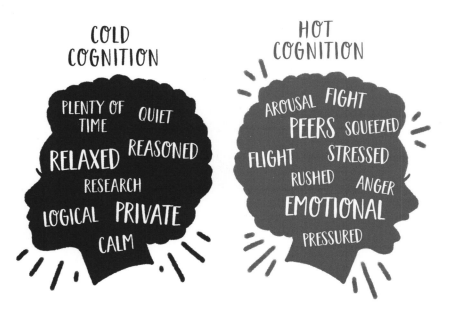

COLD COGNITION

PLENTY OF TIME   QUIET
RELAXED   REASONED
RESEARCH
LOGICAL   PRIVATE
CALM

HOT COGNITION

AROUSAL FIGHT
PEERS SQUEEZED
FLIGHT   STRESSED
RUSHED   ANGER
EMOTIONAL
PRESSURED

DO YOUNG PEOPLE HAVE ENOUGH POLITICAL KNOWLEDGE?

Another argument against lowering the voting age is that teens lack political maturity or knowledge. This is a familiar argument, as it was used for decades to bar black people and women from voting.

The political knowledge of different populations has been studied closely. Assessments out of Rutgers University suggest that sixteen- and seventeen-year-olds are just as informed, know as much about government, and pay attention to the news with similar frequency as the eighteen-to-twenty-five-year-olds who currently have the right to vote. "If you look at the kind of preparation that adolescents have to vote in terms of their understanding of issues, what they understand about civic life, their levels of participation in public life, they are not different from those we have seen in eighteen- and nineteen-year-olds," says researcher Daniel Hart, professor of childhood studies and psychology at Rutgers. "There is really no good reason to allow eighteen-year-olds to vote and exclude sixteen-year-olds."

HOW MUCH EDUCATION IS SUFFICIENT TO VOTE?

Congress concluded in the Voting Rights Act of 1965 that a sixth-grade education provided "sufficient literacy, comprehension, and intelligence to vote in any election." Most sixteen- and seventeen-year-olds have long graduated sixth grade and far surpass this standard.

If anything, political engagement among teens is on the rise. Thousands start and run political groups at school. They debate current and constitutional issues in competitions and on social media. And they organize and participate in protests.

After a mass shooting took place at Marjory Stoneman Douglas High School in February 2018, students in Parkland, Florida, marshaled hundreds of thousands of people to rally to end gun violence in the March for Our Lives protests all across the country. "It's time for us to stand up and take action and hold our elected officials responsible," said David Hogg, who was a senior at the time of the shooting. Teens also rallied counterprotests in support of the Second Amendment.

Teens have shown up in impressive numbers to Black Lives Matter marches, pro-choice and pro-life rallies, the March for Science, the Women's March, and other national and local protests. Sixteen-year-old teen Kanyinsola Mercy Oye of Columbus (Ohio) Alternative High School attended the Women's March and teamed up with a classmate to organize a protest of the Muslim ban. "My parents tell me: 'Don't resist, stay quiet, and make yourself unnoticeable so you don't die,'" she said. But she persisted. "We are stronger together."

Young people engage with our government in many ways, including testifying in front of state legislatures and the U.S. Congress. James Jelin, sixteen, a junior at the Maine School of Science and Mathematics, testified before the Maine state legislators on a bill he initiated on child support payments. Teenager Diego Morris of Phoenix testified before Congress about health care and the importance of allowing access to promising new treatments.

Young people already participate directly in elections, too. They knock on doors for candidates. They contribute to candidates' campaigns, subject to the same limit of $2,800 per candidate per federal election. That means that teens can contribute thousands of dollars to support a candidate, but they can't support them with a vote.

Sixteen- and seventeen-year-olds have even stepped up to become candidates—candidates who can't cast a vote for themselves. In 2018, a half dozen Kansas teens joined the run for governor. Seventeen-year-old Tyler Ruzich, a Republican, says that "old man principles" like those held by current elected officials aren't working for the country. He also pointed out that our founders envisioned the United States as a land where citizens his age could hold positions of responsibility and authority. "You know, lots of people

PEOPLE AGES 16 AND UP CAN ALREADY...

★ TESTIFY BEFORE STATE LEGISLATURES

★ TESTIFY BEFORE THE U.S. CONGRESS

★ KNOCK ON DOORS FOR CANDIDATES

★ CONTRIBUTE MONEY TO POLITICAL CAMPAIGNS, UP TO $2,800

★ RUN FOR LOCAL AND STATEWIDE OFFICE

ask me: 'What can you, Tyler Ruzich, do for people my age?'" he said. "In [Alexander] Hamilton's time, someone my age could be commander of a frigate."

These and many other teens want to be more engaged in democracy. "They don't want to just protest and advocate; they want to vote," says Julieta Hernandez, a high school senior from Sacramento, California, who has been working to lower the voting age. "They see it as another step to accomplish what they want to see in the government."

> TEENS CAN CONTRIBUTE $2,800 TO SUPPORT A CANDIDATE, BUT THEY CAN'T SUPPORT THEIR CANDIDATE WITH A VOTE.

WOULD TEENS JUST COPY THEIR PARENTS?

Some people worry that sixteen- and seventeen-year-olds will just vote the same way their parents vote. But independent thinking is a hallmark of this stage of life, says researcher Daniel Hart of Rutgers.

A good example is Sarah Leonard, who has been voting in Hyattsville, Maryland, since she was sixteen. While deciding where to cast her vote, she never asked which candidates her parents were supporting. She researched the issues and candidates for herself. "I'm forming my own political views from what I'm learning," she says.

Concerns that young people will support only one party are also unfounded, research suggests. Young people are not yet loyal to one party, according to research by Peter Levine, a professor of citizenship and public affairs at Tufts University. Maybe that's why roughly half of millennials identify as independents politically, according to a 2014 survey by the Pew Research Center.

WOULD TEENS JUST COPY THEIR FRIENDS?

What if teens just vote the way their friends vote? That would be no different from the voting patterns we see among adults, according to Betsy Sinclair, associate professor of political science at Washington University in St. Louis and author of *The Social Citizen: Peer Networks and Political Behavior.*

Humans are social animals. Voters enter the voting booth with ideas, priorities, and convictions that are often shaped by family members, friends, neighbors, and coworkers. But one feature of our democracy is that voters make their final choices alone, in a private voting booth or by filling out a private ballot. Democracy allows all voters to use whatever information they want to make a decision. Should that courtesy extend to sixteen- and seventeen-year-olds as well?

VOTERS MAKE THEIR FINAL CHOICES ALONE, IN A PRIVATE VOTING BOOTH OR BY FILLING OUT A PRIVATE BALLOT.

LOWERING THE VOTING AGE CAN IMPROVE TURNOUT FOR ALL AGES

Perhaps the most important reason to lower the voting age: Younger voting could be great for our democracy. We face a real problem in this country with voter turnout, with much lower engagement in elections than other established democracies. Offering the vote for the first time at the age of eighteen may be a big part of the problem.

Many eighteen-year-olds are leaving home for the first time to attend college, join the military, or set up their own households. So at a time of a major life transition, when adapting to new places and new experiences, people are expected to be successful first-time voters. They have to remember to register to vote in a new place or register in their hometown *and* request an absentee ballot. Then they need to mail in an absentee ballot or get to the polls on Election Day.

> "IT COULD BE THAT 18 IS QUITE A BAD YEAR TO BE THE FIRST YEAR TO BE ELIGIBLE TO VOTE."

It's no wonder voter turnout in the United States among young adults is among the lowest in the world. Only about 40 percent of those eligible voters turn out for presidential elections, with even less (20 to 30 percent) voting in midterm or local elections. "It could be that 18 is quite a bad year to be the first year to be eligible to vote," says Peter Levine of Tufts University.

On the other hand, sixteen- and seventeen-year-olds can be easily registered and introduced to voting by parents, schools, and other communities. They can accompany parents, teachers, or their friends to polling places. This social connection can make a real difference, according to research. Young adults who lived at home with their parents were more likely to vote than those living on their own.

Voting while young can also establish a solid voting habit. People who vote in one election are more likely to vote in future elections—25 percent more likely. So chances seem good that extending the vote to young citizens would eventually lead to increased voter turnout for *all* ages.

Places that have lowered the voting age have proved this theory. When Takoma Park first lowered the voting age to sixteen, the overall voter turnout was an abysmal 10 percent. The youth turnout blew that away, with sixteen-year-olds voting at four times that rate. In the next two elections, the overall voter turnout doubled to around 20 percent while the youth vote reached 50 percent.

Sixteen-year-old Theo Shoag says this about efforts to lower the voting age in Washington, D.C., city and federal elections: "When you vote as a young person, that gets you in the mindset for voting later in life. And that is something crucial that this nation needs."

> "WHEN YOU VOTE AS A YOUNG PERSON, THAT GETS YOU IN THE MINDSET FOR VOTING LATER IN LIFE. AND THAT IS SOMETHING CRUCIAL THAT THIS NATION NEEDS."

WHO CAN LOWER THE VOTING AGE?

Efforts to lower voting ages have been locally or state focused. In thirteen states and Washington, D.C., advocates can work directly with their towns or cities to lower the voting age for any type of election through something called a charter amendment. Basically, the local governing body has to amend the current rules to lower the voting age. No other effort would be required.

In the other states, advocates need to either change state law or get approval from the state legislature for a local change. So the first step is deciding at what level—state or local—to make the change and who has the power to implement it.

Whether working for local or state-level change, chances are good that advocates will need to educate the public and politicians and rally support. This might entail recruiting friends, neighbors, family members, and classmates; writing letters to the editor; making a website about the initiative and arguments in support of it; creating a social media campaign; gathering signatures for a petition; setting up meetings with school board members, town or city council members, or state legislators; and preparing and giving speeches.

Research, data, and passion can help convince people. But so can the equity principle: Is it fair to hold citizens age sixteen and seventeen to a higher standard than current voters? When the town council in Hyattsville, Maryland, considered lowering the local voting age to sixteen, one council member joked: "I'd like you to add an amendment . . . for a 'Clean Your Room' precondition before you grant the franchise." Everyone laughed.

But the measure passed without amendment.

Perhaps the time has come to welcome the rest of the 8 million sixteen- and seventeen-year-olds fully into our democracy—whether their rooms are clean or not.

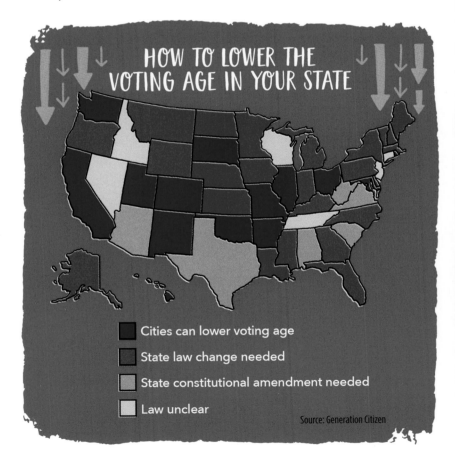

HOW TO LOWER THE VOTING AGE IN YOUR STATE

- Cities can lower voting age
- State law change needed
- State constitutional amendment needed
- Law unclear

Source: Generation Citizen

YOUNG CHANGE-MAKERS

Oliver York took up the youth vote campaign in 2014 when he was fifteen years old. "More than half of all the San Francisco ballot measures directly affect young people like me," he recalls. "But we had no say." He turned to the San Francisco Youth Commission, which advises city officials. He and a group of teens from the commission spoke to the school board. The board was so impressed that it endorsed the measure unanimously. And that was just the beginning. "We've had students meeting with legislatures. We've had students going out and knocking on doors. And we have students leading conversations with their high schools about why voting matters," York says. After two years of work, the teens got the proposal to lower the voting age to sixteen on the city ballot.

The first polls showed that only about a third of the population supported the measure. But the young people kept at it. Advocate Lorelie Vaisse says, "When people see me—a 16-year-old—civically engaged they think, 'Well, you're probably an exception.' But I'm not! There are so many 16- and 17-year-olds who are excited about voting."

In 2016, Proposition F lost by a hair. Almost half of the voters, more than 170,000 people, supported the measure.

The group is going to try again in 2020. "Young people are truly interested in this idea, and there is definitely a large group of youth willing to move it forward," says Lowell High School sophomore and campaign leader Joshua Park. "We saw time and time again that some people think this idea is a little far-fetched at first, but once you have a five-minute conversation with someone and really explain the benefits of starting voting earlier, they usually come around."

WHAT YOU CAN DO

★ Pitch the idea to friends, neighbors, family members, and classmates
★ Write letters to the editor
★ Make a website about youth voting and arguments in support of it
★ Create a social media campaign in support of the youth vote
★ Gather signatures for a petition
★ Set up meetings with school board members, town or city council members, or state legislators
★ Prepare and give speeches

WHO CAN HELP

A number of organizations offer information about youth voting and ways to get involved:

★ National Youth Rights Association offers videos, reasons to support the youth vote, updates on voting age efforts, history, and more: www.youthrights.org/issues/voting-age.
★ Generation Citizen is dedicated to the revival of civics education, including a Vote16USA effort to lower the voting age in local elections: generationcitizen.org/policy-and-advocacy/vote16usa.
★ Vote16USA is a national initiative, organized by Generation Citizen, to support youth-led campaigns to lower the voting age at local levels and promote the idea on a national

level: vote16usa.org. The website includes a toolkit to start advocating for the youth vote in your city: vote16usa.org/why-lower-the-voting-age/resource-hub.

★ #16tovote is a social media campaign. On sixteenth of every month they have a twenty-four-hour event on Twitter to raise awareness of the movement to lower the voting age. Join in by tweeting opinions, facts, graphics, stories, and links to websites, blogs, videos, and articles in support of lowering the voting age.

★ CIRCLE, the Center for Information and Research on Civic Learning and Engagement, offers detailed information on youth voting: civicyouth.org/quick-facts/youth-voting.

★ FairVote is a national organization dedicated to election reform that supports lowering the voting age: www.fairvote.org/lower_the_voting_age#why_should_we_lower_the_voting_age_to_16.

★ Unified Democracy is a political action committee devoted to increasing access to voting. Lowering the voting age is part of its platform: unifieddemocracy.org/platform.

Our country was founded on resisting taxation without representation, and yet in every election cycle, teenagers face this centuries-old disenfranchisement. Young people are our future. Lowering the voting age will help give them a voice in the democratic process and instill a lifelong habit of voting.

—CALIFORNIA ASSEMBLY MEMBER EVAN LOW (D)

Teens between 14 and 18 have far better BS detectors, on average, than 'adults' 18 and older. Wouldn't it be great if the voting age were lowered to 16?

—LAURENCE TRIBE, PROFESSOR, HARVARD LAW SCHOOL

I got to vote in 1972 because they reduced [the voting age] from 21 to 18. And they thought it was just going to upend the world, that it would be the worst thing in the world. You know, I thought I was ready at 18. I think kids know a lot more today than I knew when I was 18. And they mature a lot quicker. We screwed this place up enough already. They should take the reins of the future. I like the idea. I'd be for it.

—FORMER U.S. HOUSE REP. LUIS GUTIÉRREZ (D-ILL.)

We're all in this community together, but we still don't have a say in that. We hope that changes for the better.

—JENNY GONZALEZ, 16

When Stacey Abrams was a high school senior, a guard blocked her from the governor's mansion. She and her family had taken the bus there for Georgia's annual reception for valedictorians. Everyone else had come by car. Though she was one of the honorees, the guard asked Abrams and her family to leave. "I don't remember meeting the governor of Georgia or my fellow valedictorians," says Abrams, who is African American. "All I remember that day was a man at a gate, telling me I don't belong."

She vowed to one day return—as the governor.

In 2018, she became the first black woman nominated by a major party to run for that office. Civil rights activist Shaun King wrote on Twitter: "Black folk have lived on these lands now for 400 years. Not a single black woman has EVER served as Governor of a single state in the entire history of this nation.

That's an abomination. Ladies & Gentlemen—IT'S TIME."

Many people observe that the United States has a government run by white men. Congress, the presidency, the U.S. Supreme Court, and our state legislatures have always been, and continue to be, overwhelmingly white and overwhelmingly male compared to the rest of the country. Across local, state, and federal offices, white men, only a third of the population, are two-thirds of the candidates and hold two-thirds of the seats.

> CONGRESS, THE PRESIDENCY, THE SUPREME COURT, AND OUR STATE LEGISLATURES HAVE ALWAYS BEEN OVERWHELMINGLY WHITE AND OVERWHELMINGLY MALE.

More than half of Americans are women. But:

★ We have never elected a woman to be president or vice president.
★ Women hold fewer than a quarter of U.S. congressional seats.
★ Only nine out of fifty governors are female.
★ Twenty states have *never* had a female governor.
★ Only one state legislature in history—Nevada—has ever reached parity or majority-women status.

More than 38 percent of Americans are people of color. Yet:

★ Forty-three of our forty-four presidents have been white—all but one.

* Almost 80 percent of members of Congress are white.
* Forty-seven out of fifty governorships are held by white people.
* Thirty-seven states have *never* elected a person of color to be governor.
* At the state level, people of color hold only 14 percent of legislative seats.

Latinx and Asian Americans are the fastest-growing groups in the United States, accounting for 18 percent and 6 percent of the population. But together they hold only *2 percent* of our five hundred thousand elected offices.

A RAINBOW RIPPLE

In 2018, roughly five hundred LGBTQ candidates ran for office, an all-time record. Still, actual representation in office is only 0.1 percent of elected officials at a time when 4 to 7 percent of Americans identify as LGBTQ. (Younger people are more likely to openly identify.) Candidates hope that representation will open the eyes of people in government. "Having LGBTQ people sitting in the room while decisions are being made, and sitting there as peers, will shift the conversation," says Sharice Davids, a Native American gay woman who won a U.S. House seat representing Kansas in 2018. "It's important that the lived experiences and point of view of LGBTQ folks be included in the conversations that affect all of us."

WHY SHOULD WE CARE ABOUT DIVERSITY IN GOVERNMENT?

Diversity in decision-making is good for everyone; at least that's what research in a number of fields suggests. The consulting firm McKinsey studied 180 companies in four countries for two years and found that companies run by more racially and gender-diverse executive boards performed better financially. A study published in *Scientific American* that considered 1.5 million research papers found that papers written by more ethnically diverse teams of scientists were referred to more widely than work by more homogeneous groups, suggesting that the work of the diverse scientists was more respected by peers and more influential.

To delve deeper into the dynamics of diverse decision-making, researchers at Tufts University studied how all-white jury panels performed compared to panels of people with a range of racial backgrounds. "Diverse juries deliberated longer, raised more facts about the case, and conducted broader and more wide-ranging deliberations," reported Samuel Sommers, assistant professor of psychology at Tufts University. "They also made fewer factual errors in discussing evidence, and when errors did occur, those errors were more likely to be corrected during the discussion."

RESEARCH SUGGESTS DIVERSITY LEADS TO BETTER DECISION-MAKING.

UNREPRESENTATIVE FEDERAL GOVERNMENT

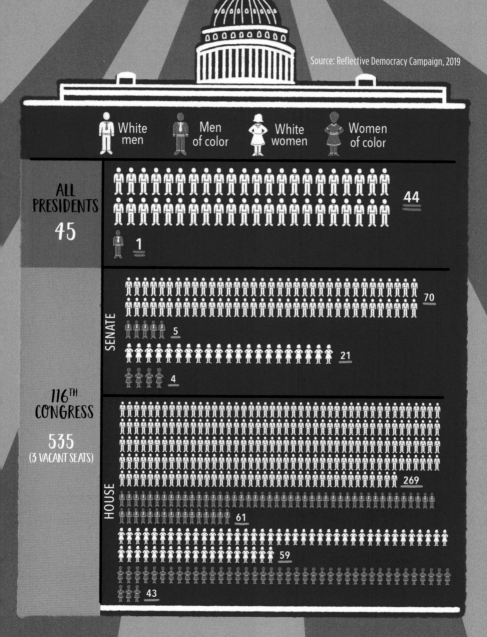

Source: Reflective Democracy Campaign, 2019

White men — Men of color — White women — Women of color

ALL PRESIDENTS 45
- 44
- 1

116TH CONGRESS 535 (3 VACANT SEATS)

SENATE
- 70
- 5
- 21
- 4

HOUSE
- 269
- 61
- 59
- 43

In reviewing recent research on diversity, *Scientific American* notes that "simply interacting with individuals who are different forces group members to prepare better, to anticipate alternative viewpoints and to expect that reaching consensus will take effort."

UNREPRESENTATIVE STATE LEGISLATURES

U.S. POPULATION	STATE LEGISLATURES
GENDER	**GENDER**
Women 51 percent	Women 29 percent
Men 49 percent	Men 71 percent
RACE	**RACE**
White 62 percent	White 86 percent
Latinx 18 percent	Latinx 4 percent
African American 13 percent	African American 9 percent
Asian American 5 percent	Asian American 2 percent
Native/Other 2 percent	

Source: New American Leaders, States of Inclusion report, 2015

MANY PERSPECTIVES

People of color bring a wide variety of perspectives to the table. In 2007, William Tong was the first Asian American to be elected to the Connecticut state legislature. He was surprised when discussions of diversity ignored Asian Americans. "Often when people speak about racial injustice, they say 'black and brown,'" he says. He recalls a colleague commenting on a bill saying, "I don't care if you are black, white, Hispanic . . ." The colleague noticed Tong and added: "or Asian."

"That was a really important moment," Tong says, "because for the first time he remembered to acknowledge that we, as a community, were there. That was a direct result of me serving on the committee, of being elected."

Lawmakers will make better laws if they take into account the experiences of people of color, many candidates say. "The people closest to the pain should be closest to the power," says Ayanna Pressley, a black woman who won a U.S. House seat representing Massachusetts in 2018.

Women also bring valuable perspectives. More women than men live in poverty and make more of the health care and education decisions in their families. They live longer, too, and thus depend more on programs such as Medicare and Medicaid. It's no surprise that a study of congressional legislation found that female legislators were far more likely to sponsor legislation on issues affecting women and children, such as women's health care coverage, child care, and sexual harassment.

Women bring more than just different priorities to lawmaking. "The message that I heard loudly from not just women across this district [was]: 'I just think it's time for more women in government, period . . . If we had more women in government, maybe things would work differently and better,'" says Susan Wild, who won a House seat representing Pennsylvania in 2018.

"THE PEOPLE CLOSEST TO THE PAIN SHOULD BE CLOSEST TO THE POWER."

Her constituents may be right. Women in Congress are particularly hardworking and effective, according to research published in the *American Journal of Political Science*. On average, compared to men, congresswomen sponsor and cosponsor more legislation. Bills they sponsor pass at higher rates than men's bills, according to a study out of Tulane University. They also bring, on average, more money (9 percent more) back to their districts than congressmen. And a recent study of 125 countries even found that governments in countries with high female representation had less corruption.

So what stands in the way of electing our very best and most diverse candidates?

> CONGRESSWOMEN SPONSOR AND COSPONSOR MORE LEGISLATION THAN MEN— AND GET MORE BILLS PASSED.

VOTERS ARE NOT THE PROBLEM

Interestingly, voters—and bias toward supporting white males—are not the problem. When Eric Gonzalez Juenke of Michigan State University looked at nearly ten thousand state elections, he found that when Latinx candidates ran for office, they won just as often as whites—even when most voters were white. A similar dynamic happens with black candidates, according to Paru Shah, associate professor of political science at the University of Wisconsin-Milwaukee. "Once minority candidates entered races, they won more than half of the elections," she wrote about her research in Louisiana.

BIAS TOWARD VOTING FOR WHITE MALES IS NOT THE PROBLEM.

Democrats and Republicans alike value the same traits in candidates regardless of gender—intelligence, honesty, confidence, and a vision for the United States, according to a 2018 poll.

So the lag in representation of women and people of color is not because voters don't want them in office.

It's because they're not on the ballot.

YOU HAVE TO RUN TO WIN

Roughly two out of every hundred Americans run for political office some time in their lives. Looking at all elections, local to federal, about 30 percent of candidates are women and just 10 percent are people of color, according to an analysis by the Reflective Democracy Campaign.

Male college students are twice as likely as female college students to consider running for public office, according to research by Jennifer Lawless, professor of politics at the University of Virginia, and Richard Fox of Loyola Marymount University. Part of the problem, they found, is that parents and teachers don't encourage females to run. But there is also a difference in the way young men and women see themselves.

College men were twice as likely as college women to believe they would be qualified for office within a few years of graduating.

Take Kirsten Gillibrand. When she was seven or eight years old, she decided she wanted to be a U.S. senator when she grew up. In her twenties, she heard a speech by First Lady Hillary Clinton that renewed her desire to run for office. A decade later she did. "It took 10 years volunteering to have the actual self-confidence to say, 'I can run for office,'" she says.

Women also cite family obligations as a barrier to running, says Lawless. Cynthia Richie Terrell, founder of Represent-Women, agrees that this needs to be tackled. "To ensure that more women can serve and lead effectively, we must address the structural obstacles that create a workplace environment unfriendly to women in Congress, state legislatures, and local offices," she says. "Legislative bodies should take action to schedule hearings and votes at reasonable times, allow for tele-commuting and tele-voting, and provide affordable and accessible child care for public servants."

In 2018, for the first time ever, the Federal Election Commission ruled that campaign funds can be used for child care. When Tammy Duckworth became the first senator to give birth while in office, the Senate unanimously voted to allow babies under age one on the Senate floor. Adjustments such as these have the potential to "shift paradigms" for females considering public office, says Debbie Walsh, director of the Center for Women and Politics at Rutgers University.

But Lawless and Fox's most powerful finding is that women are much less likely than men to be *recruited* to run for office by political parties or other interested groups. Being asked to run matters. "Potential candidates who receive the suggestion to run for office are more than four times as likely as those who receive no such support to think seriously about a candidacy," she writes.

BEING ASKED TO RUN MATTERS.

Candidates of color face similar barriers. For instance, one study showed that Asian American state representatives were twice as likely as whites to say they "never thought of running until someone suggested it." And in a study of state office holders, nearly one in every three Latinas reported being discouraged from running by someone in their party.

NO INVITATION TO THE PARTY

Maybe that's why many observers say that political parties are partly to blame. Only 62 percent of Americans are white, but more than 90 percent of Republican and independent candidates and more than 80 percent of Democratic candidates are white, according to the Reflective Democracy Campaign.

Five black female candidates who won their Democratic primaries in 2018 were surprised that they didn't even get calls of congratulation from the party organization that works to elect Democrats to Congress. "It's the height of hypocrisy," says Jeannine Lee Lake, who eventually lost her bid. "We bring millions of voters into these campaigns and we're getting no love."

"It's safe to say there are institutional barriers," says Chris Jankowski, former head of the Republican State Leadership Committee. "We've met with candidates who felt like they weren't part of the old-boy network."

"Politics is not the kind of open, competitive playing field we'd like to think of it as. It's more like trying to be inducted into a fraternity," says Reflective Democracy Campaign director Brenda Carter. "I think the number one problem is the political parties and other gatekeepers who choose candidates. I always say the parties are like hiring committees, and they're doing a really bad job of presenting voters with a range of candidates who look like the American people."

Parties often rely on fundraising ability and name recognition when identifying candidates—both areas where women and people of color may face disadvantages. Some party officials are especially leery of putting forward a candidate of color in a predominantly white district. But thirty-one-year-old Lauren Underwood (D), a black candidate who won a U.S. House seat in a predominantly white district in Illinois, believes that attitude has to change. "For so long, African Americans have only had elected representation from those traditional districts that are historically black, maybe urban. But not all of us live in all those majority-minority districts," Underwood says. "Now we are able to step forward and say, 'Hey! I grew up in this predominantly white area and my family has been here for years. I'm a leader and I have ideas.'"

WHAT IN THE WORLD?

It is difficult to compare racial diversity in governments across nations because populations vary so much around the globe. Gender equity is easier to track, and the United States lags far behind many other nations in giving women political power. Nearly one hundred countries perform better, including countries such as Bangladesh, South Africa, and Bolivia, according to the World Economic Forum's Global Gender Gap Report. Fifty-six out of 146 nations have had a female head of state in the last fifty years, according to the World Economic Forum. Countries such as India, Brazil, Chile, Israel, Norway, Germany, and the United Kingdom—and even nations with poor women's-rights records, such as Pakistan and Kyrgyzstan—have elected women as heads of state while the United States has not.

European countries that specifically work toward a target number of female candidates enjoy more gender parity, research suggests. Efforts have included the creation of a specific number of seats reserved for women, electoral laws on the gender of candidates, and commitments by political parties to support representative numbers of candidates, says Louise Davidson-Schmich, an associate professor of political science at the University of Miami. In Spain, for example, men and women are each guaranteed a minimum of 40 percent of any party's nominations. In Britain, parties sometimes nominate all-women shortlists. Use of this technique during the 1997 elections almost doubled the number of female members of Parliament, Davidson-Schmich reports.

WOMEN OF COLOR

Many potential candidates face a double whammy of barriers: barriers because of their gender and barriers because of their race. The way that multiple forms of inequality and disadvantage overlap to create additional impediments is called intersectionality. For example, black women are better educated than white women, with high voter registration and voter turnout rates, yet they are less likely to be encouraged and are more likely to be discouraged from running for office than white women or black men. If black women do stick their necks out and run, they receive fewer early endorsements and less early financial backing than other candidates. "When it comes to women of color candidates, folks don't just talk about a glass ceiling, what they describe is a concrete one," says Ayanna Pressley, the first African American woman to represent Massachusetts in Congress.

THE PROBLEM WITH INCUMBENTS

Michele Swers, a professor of political science at Georgetown University, says a big barrier to representative government is the incumbent advantage—people in office (incumbents) tend to stay in office. Historically, incumbents at all levels of government win reelection 95 percent of the time.

Why? Incumbents have name recognition. That recognition grows as they win reelection campaigns and attract media attention for their work in office. Also, campaign money flows to people already in power. Historically, U.S. House incumbents have raised four times more in campaign funding than challengers and U.S. Senate incumbents have raised eight times more than challengers, according to the Center for Responsive Politics. "It's not a talent gap, it's a financial gap," says Quentin James, cofounder of the Collective PAC, which recruits and supports progressive black candidates.

INCUMBENTS WIN REELECTION 95 PERCENT OF THE TIME.

RACISM AND SEXISM

No discussion of lack of representation of women and people of color can ignore how systemic racism and sexism affect candidates running for office. Our system of government was originally and unapologetically designed by and for white men. African American men were first granted the right to vote in 1870, but widespread voter suppression blocked many from the ballot box until the Voting Rights Act of 1965. Women were given the right to vote in 1920, just a hundred years ago. Native Americans were barred from voting until 1924. Naturalized Chinese Americans weren't allowed to vote until 1943. That is not very long ago.

Jessica Byrd advises candidates through Black Campaign School. "A lot of the strategy is similar," she says. "You have to raise money, you have to have a good message, you have to talk to every voter possible—but what's really complex is how you do that as a person who hasn't traditionally been holding power."

Candidates are too often belittled or attacked because of their race or gender or both. Asian American William Tong recalls that when he first joined the Connecticut state legislature, people frequently confused him with other people of Asian descent. People of color are often peppered with questions about the origin of their names or their background ("Where are you *really* from?") while women encounter more critiques of their appearance, mannerisms, and family life than most male candidates. During Stacey Abrams's run for Georgia governor in 2018, she faced "well-meaning folks who had opinions about my hair, my lipstick, my dresses, my shoes. I appreciate all of their input, but my hair is my hair . . . This is who I am. And I think who I am is sufficient for Georgia."

Senator Kamala Harris, a black Californian with South Asian heritage, faces and fights sexism and racism all the time.

"As a female prosecutor, let alone a woman of color, there have definitely been moments where people said, 'No, you can't do that,'" she says. "Well, I eat 'no' for breakfast, and I've never been a fan of the word 'can't'—aimed at me or anyone else."

THE MEDIA PROBLEM

Women and people of color are often treated differently than white men by the media, both in the questions they have to answer and the way they are portrayed. The nonpartisan project "Name It Change It" wants all journalists, in television, print, and online, to use the Reversibility Test: "Don't mention her young children unless you would also mention his, or describe her clothes unless you would describe his, or say she's shrill or attractive unless the same adjectives would be applied to a man. Don't say she's had facial surgery unless you say he dyes his hair or has hair plugs. Don't say she's just out of graduate school but he's a rising star. Don't say she has no professional training but he worked his way up. Don't ask her if she's running as a women's candidate unless you ask him if he's running as a men's candidate; ask both about the gender gap, the women's vote. By extension, don't say someone is a Muslim unless you also identify Christians and Jews, or identify only some people by race, ethnicity or sexuality and not others." To learn about biased media coverage and for a free (and fascinating) guide to gender-neutral media coverage, visit Name It Change It: www.nameitchangeit.org.

GETTING IN THE RACE

Number of female candidates who ran for U.S. Congress, by party

1978:
48

1998:
131

2018:
256

A RECORD!

A RECORD NUMBER OF PEOPLE OF COLOR ALSO RAN FOR CONGRESS
2018: 216

STEPPING UP

Despite these barriers, women and people of color all over the country are running for office, inspiring voters and the next generation—and winning! The 116th Congress, which began in

2019, had a record number of women—126 of 435. Candidates of color won historic firsts in 2018 too: the first two Muslim women, the first two Native American women, and the first two Latinas hailing from Texas. In fact, one third of female candidates for the House of Representatives were women of color. But the United States can't reach equal representation by fielding an equal number of candidates—we need *more* women than men to run and *more* people of color than white people to run.

WOMEN AND PEOPLE OF COLOR ALL OVER THE COUNTRY ARE RUNNING—AND WINNING.

UNOPPOSED

There's ample room in our elections for more people of color and a more diverse gender mix. More than half of elections nationwide are uncontested, meaning only one candidate is running, unopposed.

SAVE ME A SEAT

The New American Leaders Project wants political parties to look past their usual ranks to community organizations and school associations to identify candidates. They urge parties to ask and encourage people of color, LGBTQ people, and women to run, and to support them when they do.

Party leaders, political organizations, and political donors can formally commit to supporting a broader pool of candidates. We have asked other countries to commit to female representation, points out Tammy Duckworth, who has served in the U.S. House and Senate. "When the U.S. helped Afghanistan write its new constitution, we insisted they include a provision that 25 percent of their lower house of parliament be women," she says. And this was at a time when our own House of Representatives was less than 20 percent female.

Real change will take a long-term commitment. Candidates must be willing to run multiple times. Though Stacey Abrams lost her 2018 bid for Georgia governor in a tight race (49 percent to 50 percent), her quest is not over. She intends to run again, for U.S. Senate in 2020 or for governor in 2022—or perhaps even for president someday. "We will all, at some point, encounter hurdles to gaining access and entry, moving up and conquering self-doubt," she says. "But on the other side is the capacity to own opportunity and tell our own story."

WHAT YOU CAN DO

Join the Party

Ask your state's political party to set targets for female, LGBTQ, and candidates of color; to recruit candidates from beyond their active membership, from school and community organizations; to field candidates in *every* race—and to support those candidates through multiple elections. Contact your party of choice here:

State Democratic parties: asdc.democrats.org/state-parties

State Republican parties: gop.com/leaders/states

Other political parties: www.politics1.com/parties.htm

Support Diverse Candidates

Consider supporting organizations that reach out to, train, and fund female candidates, LGBTQ candidates, and candidates of color.

Women

Nominate a woman to run for office at act.myngp.com/Forms/7179724527047280384.

Learn how to run for office or how to help a woman win an election at Run to Win: www.emilyslist.org/run-to-win.

Running Start brings young women into politics by introducing them to political role models and offering training: runningstartonline.org.

VoteRunLead offers free worksheets, videos, and other tools to help female candidates decide what to run for, how to raise funds and campaign, and how to communicate with voters at voterunlead.org/resources. Women can also sign up for a half-day seminar to learn what running for office looks like or go all in with six months of training at emergeamerica.org/candidate-training.

RepresentWomen offers a toolkit to support gender parity in public office: www.representwomen.org/toolkit #handouts.

Join the effort to elect #250Kby2030 at She Should Run: www.sheshouldrun.org. She Should Run also offers free online courses on running for office and a free online course for parents or mentors of girls to help girls see themselves as leaders. You'll also find programs that develop leadership skills in girls at Teach a Girl to Lead: tag.rutgers.edu.

LGBTQ

Victory Institute trains and supports openly LGBTQ candidates, provides internships and fellowships for queer people interested in politics, and advocates for representation through presidential appointments. Visit victoryinstitute.org.

People of Color

New American Leaders supports first- and second-generation African, Arab, Asian Pacific Islander, Latinx, and Caribbean Americans to run for office at all levels. Trainings, fellowships, and a national conference focus on embracing one's heritage and immigrant experience to become a successful candidate. Support the effort or sign up to run for office: www.newamericanleaders.org.

The Asian Pacific American Institute for Congressional Studies (APAICS) offers internships, fellowships, candidate training, and information on Asian Pacific candidates: apaics.org.

The Collective PAC supports efforts to elect black candidates at every level of government. You can nominate candidates and host a fundraising party to support their efforts: collectivepac.org/about.

Latino Victory offers information, training, and funding for Latinx candidates at all levels of government: latinovictory.us.

Voto Latino offers programs to empower young Latinx to be agents of change: votolatino.org.

Native America Action is a nonpartisan political action committee that provides information about Native candidates and supports Native engagement in elections: www.nativeamerica.info.

Intersectional

Some organizations recognize that women of color face challenges because they are both women and people of color and tailor their support.

Higher Heights for America provides salons for black women to discuss political power; support for black women candidates; and the Twitter chat #SundayBrunch, where people across the country discuss issues relevant to black female leaders: www.higherheightsforamerica.org.

LatinasRepresent recruits, supports, and celebrates Latina candidates. Connect with more than thirty resources that support Latina representation or find out if there is a chapter in your area or start one: latinasrepresent.org.

The Asian American Women's Political Initiative is the only political leadership organization for Asian American women in the country. Learn more, donate, or volunteer at www.aawpi.org.

Why Don't *You* Run?

Run for Something supports millennials running for local office for the first or second time. "We want to talk to you. We don't care about your resume, your education level, or whether you've ever tweeted something stupid," the website says. "If someone is thinking about serving their community, they deserve a conversation:" runforsomething.net.

I'm not naive. I know that race is a factor, and
I know that racism is a factor. But I've always thought
once you've said that, where does it leave you?
You need a strategy to deal with it.

—FORMER U.S. SECRETARY OF STATE CONDOLEEZZA RICE (R)

It was kind of shocking to me at the time that there
would be this unwritten rule that women had to wear
dresses [on the Senate floor]. What century is this?

—CAROL MOSELEY BRAUN (D), THE FIRST BLACK FEMALE SENATOR

In my family, there were no girl chores or
boy chores. There's just things to get done.

—KRISTI NOEM (R), THE FIRST FEMALE GOVERNOR OF SOUTH DAKOTA

It is so important to remember that our diversity
has been—and will always be—our greatest source of
strength and pride here in the United States.

—FORMER FIRST LADY MICHELLE OBAMA

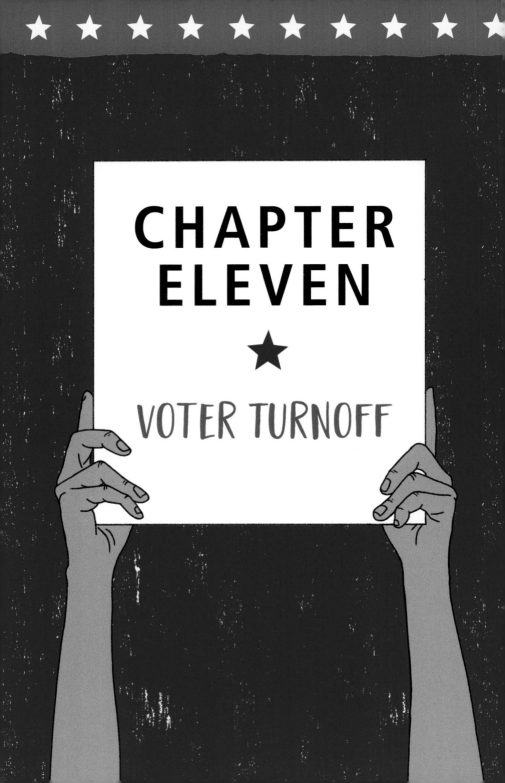

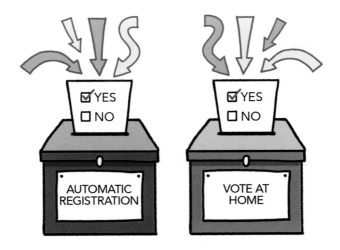

K ristin Wessell of Mt. Lebanon, Pennsylvania, volunteers to help hospital patients vote on Election Day. One year, she put on a gown and face mask to assist people in a cancer ward. A woman there said to her: "I know I'm dying and this will be my last vote."

"It made me feel like voting is a sacred duty," says Wessell.

But many Americans don't act that way. In 2014, 144 million Americans sat out the election—that's more than the entire population of Russia.

In the 2016 presidential election, 63 million voted Republican, 66 million voted Democratic. More than 100 million did not vote. If "did not vote" were a candidate, that candidate would have won in a landslide.

In 2018, less than half (49 percent) of eligible voters turned out. In fact, roughly 40 percent of eligible citizens in the United

States *never* vote their entire lives. With so little participation, can we really call this a representative democracy?

WHY EVERY VOTE COUNTS

People may think that their vote doesn't matter, but a surprising number of elections are determined by very few votes:

After the Florida recount in the 2000 presidential election, George W. Bush won by just 537 votes—and winning Florida gave him the presidency.

TURNOUT FOR THE 2016 PRESIDENTIAL ELECTION

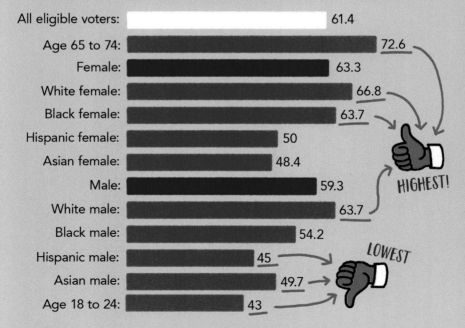

	Turnout
All eligible voters:	61.4
Age 65 to 74:	72.6
Female:	63.3
White female:	66.8
Black female:	63.7
Hispanic female:	50
Asian female:	48.4
Male:	59.3
White male:	63.7
Black male:	54.2
Hispanic male:	45
Asian male:	49.7
Age 18 to 24:	43

HIGHEST!

LOWEST

Source: Based on self-reports, which may inflate actual numbers. U.S. Census Bureau, Current Population Survey, Voting and Registration tables, May 2017 and March 2019.

WHO ARE THE VOTERS?

Black and white women and white men have the highest turnout rates overall, considerably higher than Asian and Latinx turnout.

Turnout for wealthy people (earning $100,000 or more) is 30 to 50 percentage points higher than the poor (earning less than $20,000).

The superrich, the top 1 percent, have turned out to vote at a 99 percent rate!

Turnout for older people (age sixty-five and higher) tends to be 30 percentage points higher than for young people (eighteen- to twenty-four-year-olds). In 2018, record high youth turnout for a midterm election narrowed this gap.

TURNOUT FOR THE 2018 MIDTERM ELECTION

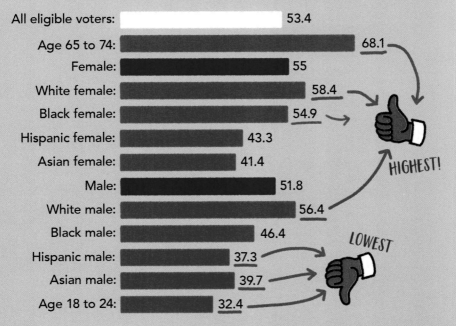

All eligible voters: 53.4
Age 65 to 74: 68.1
Female: 55
White female: 58.4
Black female: 54.9
Hispanic female: 43.3
Asian female: 41.4
Male: 51.8
White male: 56.4
Black male: 46.4
Hispanic male: 37.3
Asian male: 39.7
Age 18 to 24: 32.4

HIGHEST!

LOWEST

In 2017, David Yancey (R) and Shelly Simonds (D) tied in a race for a seat in the Virginia House of Delegates. The winner (Yancey) was determined by drawing a name from a bowl.

That same year, Colorado had seven elections that were tied and three more determined by just one vote.

Perhaps even more important, the programs, regulations, and laws of our country might be quite different if everyone voted. That's because nonvoters are a distinctive population with distinctive needs. Class is the best predictor of whether or not someone votes, according to Jan Leighley, coauthor (with Jonathan Nagler) of *Who Votes Now? Demographics, Issues, Inequality, and Turnout in the United States*. Eighty percent of high-earning Americans vote compared with less than 50 percent of low-income Americans.

The highest turnout rates are among professional salaried workers such as lawyers and executives, according to an analysis by Stanford University political scientists Adam Bonica and Michael McFaul. Turnout tends to be lowest among hourly workers in service jobs in stores and restaurants.

Nonvoters have distinct policy preferences, showing support for laws that help poorer Americans, according to research by the public policy organization Demos. On average, nonvoters are more interested in paid sick leave, free community college, a higher minimum wage, and government programs to reduce inequality. "Both nonvoters and voters support boosting spending on the poor, but nonvoter support is far stronger," the report says. "And nonvoters support the idea that government should guarantee jobs and living standards as well as take actions to reduce inequality, while voters [tend to] oppose these ideas."

Likewise, Leighley found nonvoters to be more supportive of an expanded social safety net and programs to redistribute wealth. Interestingly, nonvoters held these preferences whether they identified as Republican or Democrat.

DO NONVOTERS FAVOR ONE PARTY?

People often assume that high voter turnout would benefit the Democratic Party. But in 2018, a poll of nonvoters by Suffolk University and *USA Today* revealed that nonvoters span the political spectrum, with 17 percent identifying as liberal, 29 percent as conservative, and 36 percent as moderate.

FactCheck.org looked into the same issue. It reviewed data from the American Presidency Project and found that the highest turnout in recent history was 61 percent in 2008 when Barack Obama (D) won the presidency. The lowest turnout for a presidential election (49 percent), though, put another Democrat in office in 1996, Bill Clinton. And the second-highest turnout elected Republican president George W. Bush in 2004.

Three University of California, Berkeley, researchers similarly found that turnout does not determine the party that wins in a race. Nonvoters' leanings "fluctuate significantly across states and over time," they said.

In some ways we don't know exactly what would happen if everyone voted—but we would know that our government and its policies would more closely reflect the will of the entire nation.

THE VICIOUS CIRCLE OF ONLY FOCUSING ON VOTERS

NO VOTER OUTREACH

LABELED AS UNLIKELY VOTER

PEOPLE DON'T VOTE

Source: Nonprofit VOTE

Most Americans, voters and nonvoters alike, agree on one thing: *Everyone should vote.* Almost three-quarters of Americans surveyed by the Pew Research Center say that high turnout in presidential elections is very important. Almost all (91 percent) say voting in elections is "somewhat" or "very important" to good citizenship. And even people who are not registered or don't vote are invested in the outcome of elections. Pew found that 43 percent of unregistered voters and 59 percent of non-

A SURPRISING NUMBER OF ELECTIONS ARE DETERMINED BY VERY FEW VOTES.

voters say they care "a good deal" about who wins presidential elections.

So why don't people vote?

> **NONVOTERS HAVE DISTINCT POLICY PREFERENCES, SHOWING SUPPORT FOR LAWS THAT HELP POORER AMERICANS.**

BARRIERS TO VOTING

The number one reason citizens don't vote? They are not registered.

"I tried to register for the 2016 election," says twenty-seven-year-old Tim of Austin, Texas, "but it was beyond the deadline by the time I tried to do it."

Megan, age twenty-nine, of San Francisco explains: "I rent and move around quite a bit, and when I try to get absentee ballots, they need me to print out a form and mail it to them no more than thirty days before the election but also no less than seven days before the election." She has attempted to register. "Typically, I check way before that time, then forget to check again, or just say 'F— it' because I don't own a printer or stamps anyway."

A staggering 50 million eligible Americans are not registered. Of people who are registered, one in eight need to update their registration.

The United States is one of the only developed democracies in the world that does not automatically register citizens to vote but rather requires people to take the extra step of registering and updating their registration. The requirement to register to vote "hurts poorer and young Americans and people of color, particularly Latinos and Asian Americans," according to research by Demos.

A STAGGERING 50 MILLION ELIGIBLE AMERICANS ARE NOT REGISTERED TO VOTE.

WHAT IN THE WORLD?

Participation in elections in the United States lags far behind that in other democracies. Turnout in the United States is lower than in both our neighbors, Canada and Mexico, and most of Europe. The Pew Research Center ranked the United States twenty-sixth out of thirty-two developed democracies in election participation.

Turnout tends to be highest in countries where citizens are automatically registered to vote, such as Sweden, Denmark, and South Korea—who all enjoy close to 90 percent turnout. Universal registration "is the way most elections are run in other countries," says Richard Hasen, law professor at the University of California, Irvine.

★TURNOUT WORLDWIDE★

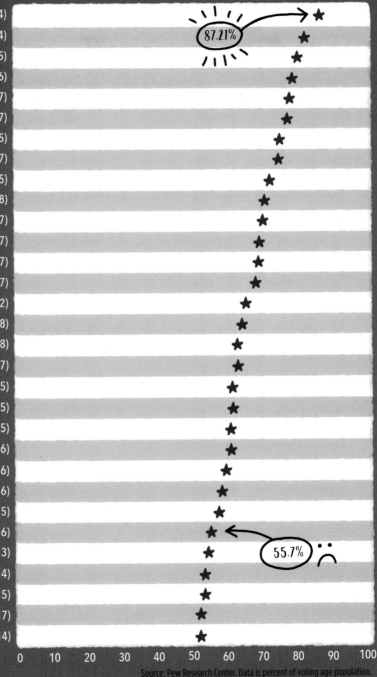

Belgium (2014) · 87.21%
Sweden (2014)
Denmark (2015)
Australia (2016)
South Korea (2017)
Netherlands (2017)
Israel (2015)
New Zealand (2017)
Finland (2015)
Hungary (2018)
Norway (2017)
Germany (2017)
Austria (2017)
France (2017)
Mexico (2012)
Italy (2018)
Czech Republic (2018)
U.K. (2017)
Greece (2015)
Canada (2015)
Portugal (2015)
Spain (2016)
Slovakia (2016)
Ireland (2016)
Estonia (2015)
United States (2016) · 55.7%
Luxembourg (2013)
Slovenia (2014)
Poland (2015)
Chile (2017)
Latvia (2014)

0   10   20   30   40   50   60   70   80   90   100

Source: Pew Research Center. Data is percent of voting age population.

LACK OF KNOWLEDGE

Some people fear they don't know enough about the voting process, the candidates, or the issues to vote. Even though twenty-three-year-old Reese of Hudson, Ohio, studied political science in college, she "never felt certain enough to vote." Indeed, in a recent survey, two-thirds of nonvoting college students cited lack of information rather than lack of interest as an explanation for why they didn't vote. They reported confusion about the voting process, deadlines, and residency rules. "Everyone is promoting registering to vote," says twenty-eight-year-old Nathan of San Diego. "But it's never how to vote or the steps to voting or what you do next after you've registered to vote. After that, it kind of just drops off and you're left in the dark, like, I don't know what to do next, you know?"

This is not just a problem that college students face. A study out of Tufts University found that almost 20 percent of working-class youth said they didn't think they knew enough to vote. And the Pew Research Center found that six out of ten intermittent voters of all ages don't vote because they don't know enough about the candidates.

Finally, Election Day itself is part of the problem. While nearly every other democracy celebrates Election Day as a holiday or holds it on a weekend, our federal Election Day is set at the first Tuesday of the month. Tuesday is a weekday, when most adults are working. "It is very hard to get voters' attention," says Elaine Kamarck, of the Brookings Institution, a public policy research group. "We squeeze our Election Day into the middle of everything else Americans are doing. We never say, 'Stop, think about your country, and vote.'"

Forcing everyone to vote on one day poses challenges as well. Whatever day is chosen will not work for some citizens. And sending everyone to polling places on the same day is a recipe for long lines and aggravation.

So what can we do?

NEARLY EVERY OTHER DEMOCRACY CELEBRATES ELECTION DAY AS A HOLIDAY OR HOLDS IT ON A WEEKEND.

BOOST PARTICIPATION

A number of election reforms—such as early voting, opening more polling places, reversing voter suppression laws, and moving Election Day to a weekend or making it a holiday—hold promise for boosting voter turnout. But two reforms stand out for their potential to quickly and thoroughly kick citizen participation up to representative levels: automatic voter registration and postage-paid vote by mail, also known as vote at home.

If these two reforms passed nationwide, every eligible citizen would be automatically registered to vote, most scheduling and accessibility barriers to voting would be overcome, the process would be simplified and easy to understand, and everyone would have ample time to research candidates and issues on their own schedule.

AUTOMATIC VOTER REGISTRATION

In 1993, Congress passed the National Voter Registration Act, also known as the Motor Voter law. It requires states to offer voter registration at motor vehicle departments and other government services.

But there is a big problem: Every state handles voter registration differently and not all states comply with the federal law. While seventeen states and Washington, D.C., automatically register and update registrations of drivers electronically, others have fallen short. They don't make it clear that people can register on the spot. They require people to fill out separate forms asking for duplicate information, and they fail to automatically update registration information, such as a change of address.

If all states reach even 75 percent compliance with the Motor Voter law, 18 million more people would be registered to vote in just two years, according to a study by Demos.

An even better approach would be to have voter registration happen automatically, with no additional work required of citizens. "A key flaw in the U.S. elections system is that the burden of registration rests on citizens rather than the government," according to Demos. "Automatic Voter Registration (AVR) would hold the government responsible for registering citizens, thereby ensuring that no one who wants to vote is turned away at the polls."

AUTOMATIC VOTER REGISTRATION COULD GET MORE THAN *50 MILLION* NEW VOTERS INVOLVED IN ELECTIONS.

Oregon passed automatic voter registration in 2016. In just a year, more than a quarter of a million new voters were automatically added to the rolls, including many black, Latinx, Asian American, and young people. More than one hundred thousand of these new voters cast a ballot.

"Studies of voter registration systems around the world and recent reforms in the United States suggest that automatic voter registration can significantly increase registration rates and enhance turnout," says Wendy Weiser of the Brennan Center. "And it can do so while improving [the accuracy of voter rolls], reducing the potential for fraud, and saving states money."

The country is already moving in this direction, with automatic voter registration being embraced both in more conservative states such as Georgia and West Virginia and in more liberal ones. Massachusetts recently passed an AVR law in time for their citizens to register for the 2020 elections. "Automatic Voter Registration will make voting more accurate, more secure, and more available to all. That's good for democracy, for election security, and for voters," says Pam Wilmot of the nonpartisan group Common Cause Massachusetts. "Utilizing existing technology to modernize the voter registration process is just basic common sense."

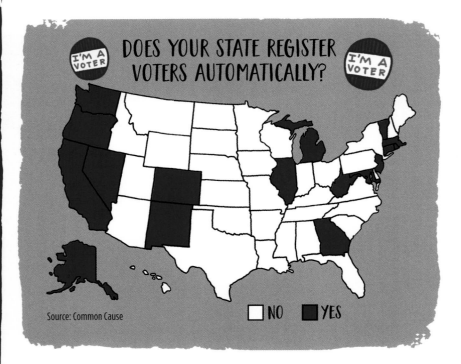

DOES YOUR STATE REGISTER VOTERS AUTOMATICALLY?

I'M A VOTER

I'M A VOTER

Source: Common Cause

☐ NO ■ YES

SAME-DAY REGISTRATION

With or without automatic registration, citizens should be allowed to correct or update their registration on Election Day—so they are *never* blocked from voting. Sometimes people get energized by campaign efforts in the last days of an election season. Same-day registration can harness this energy by letting these citizens show up, register, and vote in one trip. "Some states have been doing this since 1979," says University of Wisconsin political scientist Barry Burden. "We know [same-day registration] works quite well." Nonprofit VOTE found that citizens in states with Election Day registration turned out at rates 12 percentage points higher than in states without it.

VOTE AT HOME

In 2016, Cynthia Perez of Phoenix, Arizona, waited in line for three hours to vote. Amanda Stephens of Corpus Christi, Texas, tried two polling places. Both had long waits, so she gave up and never voted. Compare that with the experience of David Roberts, who lives in Washington State, where elections are conducted by mail. "I got my ballot in the mail several weeks before the election. One night the following week, after dinner, my family gathered around the dining room table. On one side, we had our ballots. On the other, we had Washington State's official voter guide, along with several informal voting guides from some of our favorite publications and people," he says. "We went through the ballot vote by vote—president, governor, on down to ballot initiatives on carbon taxes and public transit—discussing the opposing arguments, allowing the boys (eleven and thirteen) to ask questions. Overall, it took about an hour. When we were done, we put our ballots in a special envelope, affixed stamps, and dropped them in the mailbox. That's it."

Twenty-two states conduct some elections by mail. Three—Colorado, Oregon, and Washington—conduct all elections by mail, though ballots can be dropped off at a ballot drop location as well. David's experience is typical. An election office mails out ballots several weeks before Election Day. On their own time, in a place of their choosing, using any tools they need to research candidates or issues, citizens mark their ballots. (Some people even host voting parties with friends.) When they are done, voters put the ballot in an envelope, sign an affidavit on the outside of the envelope, and return the ballot via mail. Ballots must be postmarked on or before Election Day or dropped at collection sites.

Voting by mail makes voting accessible for seniors, working families, disabled Americans, and young voters. Everyone can vote comfortably at the time and place that works best for them.

Election officials may also send a nonpartisan voters' guide and postcard reminders to return the ballot. "Each additional communication improved the odds of voting by 4 percent," according to research conducted by Elizabeth Bergman, a political scientist at California State University, East Bay.

Sam Reed (R) served as secretary of state when Washington adopted vote by mail. Phil Keisling (D) held the same office in Oregon when it made the switch. "Each of us has faced fierce criticism from our respective party colleagues for promoting a reform that would supposedly advantage our partisan foes," they wrote. "And within each major party are factions that clearly prefer low-turnout elections, especially in party primary contests." But both officials are pleased with the results and would like to see the approach adopted nationwide.

In their states, turnout of registered voters at midterm and primary elections skyrocketed to 70 percent. Presidential elections are even more impressive. "Had every state matched our 80 percent turnout of active registered voters, 15 million more votes would have been cast nationwide" in the 2016 election, they found. Costs fell and voter fraud was virtually nonexistent. "Polling place lines? Gone. Photo ID laws? Rendered moot," they report. "Election integrity is ensured by checking every voter's signature on the return envelope against voter registration records."

> ## VOTING BY MAIL MAKES VOTING ACCESSIBLE FOR SENIORS, WORKING FAMILIES, DISABLED AMERICANS, AND YOUNG VOTERS.

Those who try vote by mail tend to prefer it, according to Bergman of California State University, East Bay. In her survey of people who'd previously voted in a polling place, but who gave vote by mail a try, 78 percent said they planned to vote by mail in the next election.

"It felt deliberative, civilized, like the way human beings ought to vote," says David Roberts, the Washington voter.

GET OUT THE VOTE!

In addition to supporting these essential reforms, we can all encourage other citizens to vote. "A wide swath of research shows that if you are contacted in advance of an election, you are more likely to vote," says Wendy Weiser of the Brennan Center. For instance, Anthony Fowler of the University of Chicago found that reaching out to people who don't usually vote increases turnout by 7 to 8 percentage points.

Political science professors Donald Green of Columbia University and Alan Gerber of Yale University reviewed forty-five studies on get-out-the-vote efforts, such as sending postcards, calling, or knocking on doors. They found some practices to be particularly powerful. Face-to-face and one-on-one is most effective, says Green. He suggests you share your interest in the election, your own desire and reasons for voting, and your own hope and desire that they vote. Highlight what is at stake and discuss closely contested races or ballot measures. Ask people to describe their voting plan. Those who can visualize themselves voting are more likely to vote.

You don't even have to be part of an official get-out-the-vote effort. People respond better to friends, neighbors, and community agencies they are familiar with. "Maybe the most effective is a close friend or coworker who says: 'Let's walk to the polls together,'" says Green.

Finally, time your efforts to the final weeks and days of the election. Election Day reminders can boost turnout by 10 percentage points.

Reaching out to potential voters can be more powerful than you might imagine. Research suggests that voting is contagious. If you persuade one new voter to participate, that person will likely influence at least one friend or family member to vote. Even better, the effort you put in for any election can last over many elections. "Thirty to 50 percent of people who turn out due to get-out-the-vote efforts in one election will continue to vote in future elections," says Kelly Born, who is in charge of democracy-related grants at the William and Flora Hewlett Foundation.

VOTE BECAUSE YOU CAN

Voting is a freedom that not everyone in the world enjoys. All around the world and throughout recent history, people have had to fight for the right to vote. Women in Switzerland were given the vote for the first time *in 1971.* Even today, women in Afghanistan, Pakistan, Uganda, Egypt, Oman, and Kenya are barred from voting or face violence if they show up at the polls.

Saudi Arabian women were granted the right to vote in 2015, but they don't get to vote very often. Elections in Saudi Arabia are rare, with just over a dozen in the last eighty years. And there are no elections in the countries of Brunei, Qatar, the United Arab Emirates, South Sudan, and Eritrea. That means millions of people are governed without any say about who rules them—ever.

The battle for the right to vote has been waged throughout U.S. history as well, with black people killed for simply registering to vote and women being tortured and force-fed in prison when they tried hunger strikes to win the vote. Someone struggled for your right to vote. Use it.

WE NEED YOUNG VOTERS

The fact that voting is contagious and that voting habits endure over time points to one more piece of the voter turnout puzzle—the importance of mobilizing young voters. Only half of the youth population (eighteen to twenty-nine) voted in the 2016 presidential election. Of eighteen- and nineteen-year-olds, the percentage dropped to 36 percent. Compare that with 70 percent of people age seventy and over.

TEACH YOUR CHILDREN WELL

Young people are 40 percent more likely to vote if they are taught about elections and voting, according to recent research. Simply showing high school students how to use a voting machine raised the chance that eighteen-year-olds would vote by *19 to 24 percentage points*. The same would probably also be true about showing them how to fill out a vote-at-home ballot. High schools could also build voter confidence by helping young people explore local, state, and national candidates and issues.

Some recent research has pinpointed particularly effective ways to mobilize young voters. Engaging them in long, loose conversations about elections, issues, candidates, and the importance of voting works best. Text and internet outreach can be effective, too, but only if it's interactive. It helps to offer practical information about voting, such as when, where, and how. Show a sample ballot. Arrange transportation if needed.

Young people have the power to transform our democracy, but only if they are fully engaged. That's why in 2018, the student leaders of Marjory Stoneman Douglas High School organized voter registration drives in all twenty-seven congressional districts in Florida, with an emphasis on the youth vote. They didn't tell people who or what to vote for—just asked them to please vote. "Four million people turn 18 this year," says Stoneman Douglas activist Cameron Kasky. "If every single one of those people votes, encourages their friends to vote, makes sure their family is getting to the polls, we can make real change in this country."

WHAT YOU CAN DO

Register and Pledge to Vote

★ Learn the preregistration laws in your state and get involved in the effort to mobilize eighteen- and nineteen-year-olds at www.18by.vote.

★ Pledge to vote, wherever you are, whenever you are eligible. You can even sign up to get reminders before you turn eighteen: yvoteny.org/?page_id=588.

Support Automatic Voter Registration (AVR)

★ Find out if your state offers automatic voter registration and learn about current efforts to implement the change at the Brennan Center's AVR page: www.brennancenter.org/analysis/automatic-voter-registration.

★ Sign a petition for national automatic registration at actionnetwork.org/petitions/sign-the-petition-support-universal-automatic-voter-registration?.

Support Same-Day Registration

★ Find out if your state offers Election Day registration at www.ncsl.org/research/elections-and-campaigns/same -day-registration.aspx.

★ Learn about and join current efforts to promote same -day registration at www.projectvote.org/issues/voter -registration-policy/same-day-registration.

Support Vote at Home

★ Encourage your members of Congress to support the national Vote by Mail Act and track its progress at www .govtrack.us/congress/bills/115/s1231.

★ Sign a petition in support of national vote by mail at www .signherenow.org/petition/national-vote-by-mail.

Share Knowledge

★ Ask your school district or school to offer Rock the Vote's free forty-five-minute class on elections—or teach it on your own! Get the curriculum at www.rockthevote.org/ resources/democracy-class.

★ Some nonvoters fear they don't know enough to vote wisely. Empower them by sharing nonpartisan voter guides: campuselect.org/voter-education/candidate-issue-guides.

Until AVR: Register New Voters

★ Learn the rules for voter registration in your state, including whether you need training and how to request and submit forms, at nationalvoterregistrationday.org/partner-tools/rules-for-voter-registration-drives.

★ Get a voter registration toolkit at marchforourlives.com/host-your-own-voter-registration-toolkits.

★ Rock the Vote offers a free guide to running your own voter registration drive, including Rock the Vote logos and a social media guide: www.rockthevote.org/action-center/host-your-own-event.

★ Download a free social media kit to encourage registration and voting: campuselect.org/wp-content/uploads/2018/ . . ./CEEP-Social-Media-Toolkit.pdf.

★ Sign up to register voters at concerts and other events at headcount.org.

Get Out the Youth Vote

★ Start your own youth get-out-the-vote effort at leadasap.ysa.org/ideas/help-get-out-the-vote.

★ Mobilize your college or university to encourage voting. The Campus Vote Project offers a free Student Engagement Handbook to get you started: compact.org/resource-posts/student-voter-engagement-handbook.

★ Also check out their Best Practices to Help Students Register and Vote: campusvoteproject.org/wp . . ./Best-Practices-for-Colleges-and-Universities-2015.pdf.

★ This checklist breaks down recommended steps to take: www.studentslearnstudentsvote.org/the-checklist.
★ One way to engage and educate your friends and family is by covering the election yourself on your social media platforms. Find out how with this free guide: campuselect .org/wp-content/uploads/2017/12/covering_elections_ through_social_media_reporting.pdf.

Make Voting Memorable

Getting out the vote can be fun. Here are some ideas:

★ Gather a crowd using a flash mob or street theater and then pass out registration and voting information. Florida State University students gathered in the student union wearing T-shirts with the election date and voting slogans. They froze in position for five minutes so people could read the messages and then moved on to do the same at different locations around campus.
★ Make a mural or decorate a sidewalk with chalk with messages about voting. Have passersby join in by writing why they vote, what issues they care about, and so on.
★ Lots of people knock on doors during Halloween, which falls just before Election Day. Instead of asking for candy, hand out candy and voting information as part of a Trick or Vote campaign. Learn more at campuselect.org/get-out -the-vote/trick-or-vote.
★ Host a Vote Together party. Get ideas at votetogetherusa.org.

Change is hard. And if you don't fight for it,
you can't win. But change can happen.

—U.S. SENATOR ELIZABETH WARREN (D-MASS.)

We do not have a government by the majority. We have
government by the majority who participate.

—THOMAS JEFFERSON (DEMOCRATIC-REPUBLICAN),
THIRD U.S. PRESIDENT

If we are to maintain the principle that governments
derive their just powers from the consent of the governed,
if we are to have any measure of self-government, if the
voice of the people is to rule, if representatives are truly
to reflect the popular will, it is altogether necessary
that in each election there should be a fairly
full participation by all the qualified voters.

—CALVIN COOLIDGE (R), THIRTIETH U.S. PRESIDENT

The biggest hurdle that our communities have is
cynicism—saying it's a done deal, who cares, there's
no point to voting. If we can get somebody to care,
it's a huge victory.

—ALEXANDRIA OCASIO-CORTEZ (D),
MEMBER OF CONGRESS REPRESENTING NEW YORK

CHAPTER TWELVE

★

LET'S FIX OUR DEMOCRACY!

Americans are blessed to live in a country that allows us so much freedom. We enjoy the right to free speech, the right to gather with others, and the right to air our grievances to our government. These freedoms underpin the greatest strength of our democracy—that it was designed to evolve as the will of the people evolved. And evolve it has. Over the last few hundred years, our democracy has been transformed many times, but only when the people demanded it.

We have every right, and every tool we need, to form a more perfect union, to come closer to the ideal of one person, one vote, to fully realize a government by and for the people.

But reform does not happen on its own. It takes the power of people just like you.

So what can *you* do to help our democracy truly represent us all?

WHO WILL BENEFIT FROM REFORM?

Almost all Americans have been hurt by flaws in the system and almost all Americans will benefit from reform:

★ Enacting a national popular vote would give citizens in more than *forty spectator states* a real say in the election of our president and vice president.

★ Voters in *more than half of the states* would benefit from taking redistricting out of the hands of politicians and putting it into the hands of citizens or another neutral body.

★ Citizens in *half of the states* would gain access to voting by ending voter suppression.

★ Reducing the role of money in elections and lawmaking would give power to the *99 percent* of Americans who are not extremely rich. And it would shift political power from industries and corporations to ordinary citizens.

★ Restoring the vote to ex-felons would welcome *3.3 million* people back into our democracy.

★ Statehood for the District of Columbia and Puerto Rico would extend full voting rights to *4.2 million* citizens.

★ Extending the vote to sixteen- and seventeen-year-olds would give *8 million citizens* who can already hold jobs, pay taxes, get married, and drive on public roads the right to vote on issues that matter to them.

★ Automatic voter registration would bring *50 million citizens* an important step closer to voting and transform voter turnout.

★ Vote by mail could make voting accessible and easy for *every citizen in the country.*

YOU CAN VOTE!

Your vote matters. If you are too young to vote now, register as soon as you can. If you don't usually vote or have never voted before, please register. The country needs to hear your voice.

Chances are good that you will be offered the chance to vote not only on issues you care about but on democracy reform itself. Many states are considering various prodemocracy laws and amendments, and many of these issues may end up on state ballots. Likewise, candidates who support or oppose democracy reform may be running locally, statewide, or nationally. Your vote can put reformers in office.

So please vote—in the next election and every election thereafter. Talk with your friends and neighbors about these issues and encourage them to vote too.

But there's so much more you can do to help fix our democracy. You don't have to wait until Election Day to have your voice heard.

FIND YOUR REPRESENTATIVES

★ U.S. Senator

★ U.S. Senator

★ U.S Representative

★ State Legislator

★ State Legislator

To identify the members of Congress and state legislators who represent you and to find their phone numbers and addresses, go to www.270towin.com/elected-officials and type in your zip code at "Who Represents Me?" Click the icons to follow your representatives on Facebook, Twitter, and other social media and to link to their websites, which have lots of useful background information.

Remember that you may need to update these contacts after elections if your representatives have changed.

FIVE IMPORTANT NAMES

There are five lawmakers whose job is to represent *you*. A powerful and easy first step is to add their five names to the contact list on your phone or computer. For the U.S. Congress, add the contact information for the two U.S. senators who represent your state and the one member of the U.S. House of Representatives who represents your district. For state-level policy, add the state legislators who represent you, usually two people. Collecting this important contact information for your representatives should take less than half an hour, and will arm you to be ready to make our representative democracy work better for you—and all of us.

ONE ISSUE OR THE WHOLE SHEBANG?

Did one issue—such as voter suppression, gerrymandering, or the youth vote—really rouse you? If so, focus your attention there. Mari Copeny, who began advocating for clean water in Flint, Michigan, when she was only eleven, says this: "Think about what really matters the most to you and go for it. It's easy to fight for things that are close to your heart." Resources at the end of each chapter will link you to information about the issue and connect you with organizations already working to fight for change.

"THINK ABOUT WHAT REALLY MATTERS THE MOST TO YOU AND GO FOR IT."

Many flaws in the system are interconnected, though, affecting the functioning of our democracy as a whole. Instead of focusing on just one issue, you could advocate for a bundle of reforms all designed to improve our democracy. New laws often include a number of different parts,

★ 235

so you can push for a slate of reforms, including fixing the Electoral College, gerrymandering, the influence of money, voter suppression, voter registration, and the like.

Legislators are already considering these issues together. In 2019, Oregon senator Jeff Merkley (D) unveiled a blueprint to restore American democracy, including proposals to take on voter suppression, gerrymandering, dark money, and unequal representation in our democracy. "We will be unable to address the big challenges we face as a nation—the ones that determine [whether] the America we leave our children creates more opportunity for a brighter future than the one we inherited—until we boldly and decisively reform our democracy," he says. The bill hasn't moved in the Senate but the U.S. House passed H.R. 1, the For the People Act, which would require automatic voter registration nationwide, expand early voting, outlaw gerrymandering, restore the right to vote to all people who have served sentences, and require disclosure of donations to super PACs and other outside spending groups.

These efforts suggest that citizens may have success advocating for our democracy as a whole.

"WE WILL BE UNABLE TO ADDRESS THE BIG CHALLENGES WE FACE AS A NATION UNTIL WE BOLDLY AND DECISIVELY REFORM OUR DEMOCRACY."

THE POWER OF *YOUR* STATE

While people often obsess about who is president or which party controls Congress, the truth is that we can fix much of what ails our democracy at the state level. You may have noticed that most of the flaws in our democracy—gerrymandering, voter suppression, and felon voting laws—are the result of problems with election laws *at the state level*. Article 1, Section 4 of the U.S. Constitution gives states responsibility for setting the rules governing federal elections. They control state elections, too. Though Congress can overrule states, it is not inclined to interfere with state policy unless there is a great nationwide groundswell to do so. So your state legislature is a great place to start.

HOW GREAT IS MY STATE?

To find out how your state fares on the issues covered in this book, visit the Democracy State-by-State page of the website at youcallthis.com. The page also offers links to model legislation on all the issues.

Statewide change has already begun. In 2018, measures to reduce the influence of money and corruption passed in Florida, Massachusetts, Missouri, New Mexico, and North Dakota. Anti-gerrymandering laws passed in Colorado, Michigan, Ohio, and Utah. Floridians restored the vote to more than a million ex-felons. Citizens in Maryland passed same-day registration, and voters in Nevada passed automatic voter registration.

Another great reason to work for reform at the state level is that state legislatures tend to be much more responsive and more productive than Congress. One study showed that state legislatures are six times more productive at passing bills than Congress.

WE CAN FIX MUCH OF WHAT AILS OUR DEMOCRACY AT THE STATE LEVEL.

ACT LOCAL, TOO!

Remember, too, that you can fight for change locally. In 2018, citizens passed prodemocracy measures—addressing issues such as corruption and gerrymandering—in Baltimore, Maryland; Denver, Colorado; New York City; Phoenix and Tempe, Arizona; and Long Beach and Santa Barbara, California.

Also note that people who serve as mayor or on city councils, town committees, or neighborhood commissions can not only make some of these reforms happen locally—they might also someday rise to become the governor or a member of the state legislature or Congress where they will have more power to press for reform.

You can find your mayor at www.usmayors.org /mayors. Type in the name of your town or city and the word *government* to find the web pages that will connect you with other local representatives.

IF STATES CHANGE, THE COUNTRY FOLLOWS

The effort you put into reforming your state can also trigger nationwide reform, according to a fascinating study by the news organization Bloomberg. The reporters found that "social change in the U.S. appears to follow a pattern: A few pioneer states get out front before the others, and then a key event—often a court decision or a grassroots campaign reaching maturity—triggers a rush of state activity that ultimately leads to a change in federal law."

For example, Wyoming was the first state to grant women the right to vote. Over the next decade, only three more states joined in. Then things really shifted at the state level. Between 1910 and 1919, twenty-three more states made the change. The U.S. Congress responded to this groundswell by proposing the Nineteenth Amendment, extending the right to vote to all women.

Bloomberg found similar patterns with interracial marriage, prohibition (of alcohol), the pro-choice movement, and gay rights. "Though the pattern of social change may have remained largely the same over the years, change is happening faster now," the report says.

This suggests, powerfully, that your efforts in your state, joined with the work of citizens in other states, could trigger nationwide change.

WHAT ABOUT CONSTITUTIONAL AMENDMENTS?

Yes, amending the U.S. Constitution is difficult, requiring support from two-thirds of both the U.S. House and Senate and ratification by thirty-eight of fifty state legislatures. But it's not like we've never amended it. The United States has amended its constitution twenty-seven times, most recently in 1992.

Many believe passing constitutional amendments is worth the effort. The reform group Citizens Take Action says: "Though passing a constitutional amendment may sound like an almost unprecedented step, nearly every generation of Americans except ours has done it! We are the only ones who haven't used this valuable tool and it's time for us to get to work because the fate of our democracy is too important to leave in limbo."

But here's an even more promising route: state constitutions. States routinely amend and rewrite their constitutions. In many states, voters can amend the state constitution through ballot measures. "Each state has its own constitution, and the typical state has had three constitutions," says Sanford Levinson, a constitutional law professor at the University of Texas Law School. "A couple of them have had 10 or 11. There've been about 235 state constitutional conventions and zero new national conventions since 1787." So while you can think nationally, you might have more success, more quickly, working for state constitutional amendments to reform our elections.

WHAT INFLUENCES REPRESENTATIVES?

ACCORDING TO REPRESENTATIVES...

IN-PERSON VISITS
FROM CONSTITUENTS: **94%**

INDIVIDUALIZED EMAIL: **92%**

INDIVIDUALIZED LETTER: **88%**

LETTER TO EDITOR
OR EDITORIAL: **87%**

Source: Based on surveys of congressional staff conducted by the
Congressional Management Foundation

REACH OUT TO YOUR REPRESENTATIVES

The most powerful way to fight for change is to advocate for reform through your representatives, research suggests. "Better policy decisions are made through better citizen advocacy," according to a report by the Congressional Management Foundation (CMF) called "Citizen-Centric Advocacy." "This research proves that [citizens'] voices *do* make a difference, and they can magnify their voices by using more effective advocacy techniques."

One easy option is to email or call your representatives. Research from the CMF suggests this simple outreach from people who live in the legislators' districts, called constituents, is relatively effective. More than a third of legislative staff consider personalized email from constituents to be "very effective," according to the CMF. Almost a quarter give phone calls the same rating.

You can also post comments on a lawmaker's social media site immediately after an event or speech. These comments are noticed by legislative staff.

WHAT NOT TO DO

Don't waste time contacting representatives who are not your representatives. The hard truth is that it is not their job to listen to you. They are in office to represent the people in their state or district. "If you want democracy to work effectively and you want Congress to listen to you, you must communicate and develop relationships with those who represent you, whether or not you like them or their politics," says Kathy Goldschmidt of the CMF.

In addition, sending out mass emails with identical wording is not a great use of your time. Mass identical emails generally aren't read *or* counted. But you can make your email stand out if you personalize it. "It's really a missed opportunity," says Bradford Fitch of the CMF. "If citizens did a little more—individualizing that email and talking about how their family, or their business, or their trade group is affected in their community, that is what members of Congress are looking for when interacting with citizens."

Attend town hall meetings put on by your representative and ask questions. Letters to the editor also have influence on lawmakers' decisions, according to the CMF.

THE MOST POWERFUL TECHNIQUE

There is one form of citizen advocacy more powerful than the rest. "Our research has shown that building relationships—emphasizing quality over quantity—is more effective at influencing lawmakers," according to the CMF report. A stunning 94 percent surveyed say that an in-person visit from a constituent had "some" or "a lot" of influence on the lawmaker. Ninety-nine percent said meetings between their staff and constituents are "somewhat" or "very" important to help them understand citizens' views and opinions.

"In-person meetings are the easiest way for staff to understand an issue because it gives us the chance to ask questions and put a face with the issue," one legislative staff member reported.

You don't even have to travel to Washington, D.C., or your state capital to meet with your legislators. Most representatives have district offices in your area that they visit regularly.

Citizen advocate Bob O'Hara says meeting with representatives is simpler than you may think: "Each time the process is easy—call the office, set up a time, show up and make your pitch."

Here's how to do it, step-by-step.

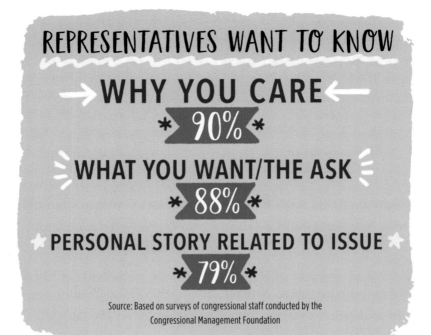

REPRESENTATIVES WANT TO KNOW

→ WHY YOU CARE ←

* 90% *

WHAT YOU WANT/THE ASK

* 88% *

PERSONAL STORY RELATED TO ISSUE

* 79% *

Source: Based on surveys of congressional staff conducted by the
Congressional Management Foundation

IN-PERSON VISITS FROM A CONSTITUENT HAVE
"SOME" OR "A LOT" OF INFLUENCE ON LAWMAKERS.

Be Prepared

In 1996, as a former staff member for the U.S. Senate Committee on Labor and Human Resources, I often met with citizen-advocates. The most effective meetings were those where the citizens were prepared, handed me helpful materials, and were specific about what they wanted the senators to do. Research conducted by CMF closely matches my own insights.

★ Call the lawmaker's office two to four weeks ahead of time to schedule a meeting. (See Find Your Representatives.)

* Search the internet to learn about the legislator. Find out a little of their personal history, especially if you can make a personal connection. Maybe you both support the same sports team, or admire the same people, or love the same kind of dog.
* Do some research to find out if the lawmaker has taken a public stand on any of the reforms you want to discuss. Be sure to thank the legislator for any previous work on the issue.
* A few days before the meeting, email the legislator's office a one- to two-page summary of what you want to talk about. This will help you and the representative and staff prepare.

Your goal is to bring the issues to life for your representative, ask for specific actions, and show them why these changes matter so much to you and your community.

At the Meeting

Most lawmakers have staff who assist and advise them. Chances are good that a staff member will attend your meeting—with or without the legislator. Don't be put off or discouraged if you only meet with staff—they are the eyes and ears of the legislator, and their job is to accurately report on the meeting. Staff can be very influential in convincing a legislator to embrace an issue. So give it your all whether or not the representative is there. Be aware that legislative meeting rooms are small. Attend with no more than one or two other people.

HOW A BILL *REALLY* BECOMES A LAW

You may have heard that a bill becomes a law when it passes the House of Representatives and the Senate and is signed by the President. The real process, which is pretty similar at the federal and state levels, has more steps:

★ Someone comes up with an idea for a new law or a change to an existing law. The idea can originate from any citizen, government worker, group of people, company or nonprofit, or elected official or their staff.

★ Someone drafts legislation. Often lawyers or legislative aides help write bill language.

★ Members of Congress (or state legislators) introduce the bill into their chamber. Other members of Congress can sign on as co-sponsors indicating support for the bill. The clock starts ticking. The bill must complete all the necessary steps in the same congressional session or it will have to be reintroduced and begin the process again.

★ The bill is assigned a number and moved to a committee or subcommittee of legislators who specialize in matters covered in the bill. The fate of most bills is sealed in committee. If committee members have interest in a bill, they hold hearings where experts and interested people testify. Committee members decide whether to debate and "mark up" or revise the bill. A majority of committee members must agree to pass the bill out of committee.

★ The bill moves to the full House or Senate. The party in the majority decides which bills will be debated and voted on and when. Some bills may never be scheduled for a vote.

★ A scheduled bill is debated, amended, and voted on subject to the rules of that chamber.

★ If the bill is passed by one chamber, it must go through the same process in the other. This can happen simultaneously or consecutively. But it must happen in the same session, which lasts just one year.

★ Any differences between bills passed by the two chambers must be resolved, often in a conference committee made up of members of both chambers. Inability to resolve difference kills the bill.

★ Once the same bill has passed both chambers, it goes to the President to sign or veto. Two-thirds of both chambers must vote to override a veto. President can also kill a bill by not signing it for 10 days if Congress is no longer in session (pocket veto).

★ The bill becomes a law if the President signs it or if it remains unsigned after 10 days if Congress is in session.

★ Any bills that have not become laws in the session must reintroduced for consideration in another session and proceed again through all the steps.

Learn more at www.usa.gov/how-laws-are-made#item-213608.

TAKING IT TO THE STREETS

The First Amendment of the U.S. Constitution protects "the right of the people peaceably to assemble, and to petition the Government for a redress of grievances." Protesting—gathering with others to publicly speak out and urge action—is a form of assembly and free speech and thus is protected by the Constitution.

Americans have been embracing this right. Since the start of 2016, one in five Americans has protested in the streets or participated in a political rally, according to Fitch of the CMF. Roughly 20 percent had never protested before.

Do these protests make any difference?

Research out of Stockholm University, the Harvard Kennedy School, and the American Enterprise Institute suggests that the larger the crowd at a protest, the more the protest affects voting in Congress. "Together our results show that protests can build political movements that ultimately affect policymaking," the researchers write.

To learn more about your rights while protesting, read the American Civil Liberties Union's guide to protesting at www.aclu.org/know-your-rights/demonstrations-and -protests?redirect=free-speech/know-your-rights-demonstrations-and-protests.

the world is run by those who show up," she says. "So show up, be present, and fight for what you believe in."

RISE UP

Try not to be intimidated by your representatives. Remember, they work for you. It is their job to listen to you. In fact, your representatives *want* to meet with you and hear your concerns. Ninety-five percent of legislators surveyed by the CMF rate "staying in touch with constituents" as a "very important" aspect of their job, crucial to their effectiveness. "Congress is actually made up of hardworking public servants who are mostly motivated by what is in the best interests of their constituents," says Fitch of the CMF. The same is also true of your state legislators.

YOUR REPRESENTATIVES WORK FOR YOU.

You will not be alone in your efforts. Citizen activism is on the rise. Nearly half of registered voters reported contacting a member of Congress within the last five years, according to a recent survey. One U.S. Senate office saw a 900 percent increase in communication from people in the district in just one year. In 2016, an average of twenty to thirty people showed up at town hall meetings, according to Fitch of the CMF. In just a year, this skyrocketed to more than 240 people per meeting.

It's okay if you have never done this before. "The hardest part was just starting," says Katie Fahey, who led the charge to dismantle gerrymandering in Michigan. "Don't be afraid to just dive in! There are a lot of great organizations that have been helping bring change for decades, so doing your research and then reaching out to contact organizations who have helped with similar issues in your or other states can be a valuable resource too. You have to set your eyes on the goal, figure out who you should bring in, and give everyone an opportunity to draw on their strengths to help you along the way."

Eighteen-year-old Madison Kimrey has been working to reform voting laws in her state of North Carolina for several years. "If we start to show we're paying attention and let our representatives and candidates know we're paying attention, the people who want to represent us are going to have to take our views into account in order to get elected," she says.

"DON'T BE AFRAID TO JUST DIVE IN!"

We often hear about problems spiraling out of control. But solutions can snowball too. "For every person who speaks up and gets involved, it can encourage another person to do the same thing," says Kimrey.

It is work that truly anyone can do. "My story could be the story of anyone who decides to do something to use their time and talents to make a difference," says Kimrey. "Pay attention, find the issues that are important to you, and take action. The world needs our beauty, the kind of beauty that comes from being true to ourselves and believing in ourselves. All it takes is one small thing to help make a difference."

Imagine the payoff. *You* can be part of fixing our democracy. Like our founders long ago, *your* work can form a more perfect union.

"Our history tells us that true power has always been in the hands of ordinary citizens," says Kimrey. "Sometimes change takes a long time, but if people continue to work for change, it will come."

RECENT WINS FOR DEMOCRACY

FLORIDA
Lobbying Restrictions
PASSED

PHOENIX, AZ
Disclosure of Contributions
PASSED

MISSOURI
Clean Elections
PASSED

COLORADO
Fair Maps
PASSED

NORTH DAKOTA
Anti-Corruption Measure
PASSED

MICHIGAN
Voters Not Politicians
Redistricting
PASSED

BALTIMORE, MD
Fair Elections
PASSED

OHIO
Fair Districts
PASSED

DENVER, CO
Democracy for the People
PASSED

UTAH
Better Boundaries
Redistricting
PASSED

MASSACHUSETTS
People Govern, Not Money
PASSED

FLORIDA
Restoring Voting Rights
to Ex-Felons
PASSED

NEW YORK CITY
Public Financing
PASSED

MARYLAND
Election Day Registration
PASSED

NEVADA
Automatic Voter
Registration
PASSED

**U.S. HOUSE OF
REPRESENTATIVES**
For the People Act
PASSED

CHECK OUT YOUCALLTHIS.COM

The website for this book, youcallthis.com, includes:

★ Information on how YOUR state fares on these issues

★ How you can get involved in YOUR state

★ Sample legislation

★ Discussion questions for book clubs and classrooms

★ Additional articles and resources

★ How to book the author for an inspiring talk about the state of our democracy

FURTHER READING

The chapter endings include useful resources that will help you learn more and get involved. Here are a few more resources you might find interesting.

BOOKS

Anderson, Carol. *One Person, No Vote: How Voter Suppression Is Destroying Our Democracy* (Bloomsbury, 2018).

Conrad, Jessamyn. *What You Should Know About Politics . . . But Don't: A Nonpartisan Guide to the Issues That Matter* (Arcade, 2016).

Kauffman, L. A. *How to Read a Protest* (University of California Press, 2018).

Koza, John R., Barry Fadem, Mark Grueskin, Michael S. Mandell, Robert Richie, and Joseph F. Zimmerman. *Every Vote Equal: A State-Based Plan for Electing the President by National Popular Vote.* Available for free download at www.every-vote-equal.com.

Lepore, Jill. *These Truths: A History of the United States* (W. W. Norton & Company, 2018).

Levinson, Cynthia, and Sanford Levinson. *Fault Lines in the Constitution: The Framers, Their Fights, and the Flaws That Affect Us Today* (Peachtree, 2019).

Loewen, James. *Lies My Teacher Told Me: Everything Your American History Textbook Got Wrong* (New Press, 2018).

Page, Elisa Camahort, Carolyn Gerin, and Jamia Wilson. *Road Map for Revolutionaries: Resistance, Activism, and Advocacy for All* (Ten Speed Press, 2018).

WEBSITES

Actionnetwork.org: Offers community organizing tools free for grassroots movements.

Ballotpedia.org: Nonpartisan, nonprofit source of information on elections and legislation.

Brennancenter.org: Issue pages cover the latest on redistricting, money in politics, voting rights, foreign influence, and election security.

Congress.gov: Search to learn more about any federal bill or law and view Congress's schedule.

Congressfoundation.org: CMF offers a terrific citizen resource center and training for citizen advocates.

Mediabiasfactcheck.com: A great place to find unbiased news sources and see how your news sources compare in terms of bias.

NationalPopularVote.com: All about the Electoral College and progress on the interstate compact for a national popular vote.

News.gallup.com: Timely polling on what people think in the U.S. and all across the globe.

OpenSecrets.org: Track campaign spending by U.S. candidates, parties, and organizations and find out who is behind dark money.

Petitions.moveon.org: Start your own online petition.

Pewresearch.org: Top-notch polling and research data and reports on U.S. politics and trends.

TO A SPECIAL GROUP OF COMMITTED PEOPLE

It took a group of dedicated people to create our democracy, it will take a group of steadfast reformers to fix our democracy, and it has taken a group of amazing, committed colleagues to write this exploration of our democracy.

This book builds on the work of so many who constantly strive to make our government work better. Thousands of researchers devote their lives and careers to tracking, analyzing, and testing countless aspects of our democracy. Pollsters interview millions of people about their thoughts and reactions to almost every issue and law. Journalists talk to countless ordinary people and public officials and pore over reports and documents to capture the stories, words, feelings, and trends of our times as they unfold. And then there are the activists, the people working every day to form a more perfect union, to demand a government of the people, by the people, and for the people. I am so grateful for all their contributions to our country and to this book.

Elizabeth Goss provided essential research, digging up articles, reports, surveys, studies, anecdotes, stories, and quotations, as well as offering vital assistance with the extensive endnotes and fact-checking. She did all this with a lively passion for the topic and good cheer. Thank you, Liz. Working with you has been a pleasure. For last minute fact-checking and vital outreach work, thanks to Claire Alongi and Gatlin Webb.

A handful of expert readers offered their comments on the manuscript in record time. Thank you to Maria Cardona, CNN/CNN en Español political commentator and founder of Latinovations; John F. Kowal, vice president for programs at the Brennan Center for Justice at NYU School of Law; Matthew Shugart, a professor of political science at the University of California, Davis, and coauthor of *A Different Democracy: A Systematic Comparison of the American System with Thirty Other Democracies;* and Deana Goldsmith Tanguay, program manager for the History and Civics Project at the University of California, Santa Cruz. What I got right is thanks to Maria, John, Matthew, and Deana; any errors are mine.

I have been blessed with loyal readers and friends in two wonderful critique groups and another group called Daily Democracy. They have plowed through drafts with all their complexities multiple times. My deep appreciation to Addie Boswell, Melissa Dalton, Ruth Feldman, Ellen Howard, Alana Kansaku-Sarmiento, Barbara Kerley, Amber Keyser, Michelle McCann, Shana Niederman, Sara Ryan, Nicole Schreiber, and Emily Whitman for their insightful comments. To my editor, Erica Zappy Wainer and the whole team at Houghton Mifflin Harcourt, thank you for taking on this thorny book and helping bring these important issues to readers. Ellen Duda, thanks for turning infographics into art!

Special thanks to the Jacob K. Javits Foundation, which supported me with a full fellowship to obtain my Master's in Public Policy and to work as a fellow in the U.S. Senate for a year. This book would not have been possible without the knowledge I gained at the Goldman School of Public Policy and the experience and insights I acquired working in the Senate.

Finally, thanks to my husband, Craig, for years of fascinating political conversations spurred by what he heard on NPR on his way home from work.

I'm so grateful to be surrounded by such a wonderful group of thoughtful, committed citizens dedicated to changing the world. You all have truly made this a better book—and me a better person.

ELIZABETH RUSCH

NOTES

For complete citations including URLs please visit the website for the book at www.youcallthis.com.

Introduction: Do You Live in a Democracy?

1

"We the People": ConstitutionUS, "The Constitution of the United States," September 17, 1787.

The founders of the United States: Encyclopaedia Britannica, s.v. "Democracy."

2

Only one in five Americans trusts: Yvote, "We Have a Crisis in Youth Voter Turnout in the United States."

When asked to compare our political system: Pew Research Center, "1. Democracy and Government, the U.S. Political System, Elected Officials and Governmental Institutions," April 26, 2018.

Millions struggle to pay the costs: Felix Richter, "The U.S. Has the Most Expensive Healthcare System in the World," *Statista,* March 23, 2017.

Forty percent of Americans: Federal Reserve, "Federal Reserve Board Issues Report on the Economic Well-Being of U.S. Households," May 22, 2018.

About 40 million Americans live in poverty: Kayla Fontenot, Jessica Semega, and Melissa Kollar, "Income and Poverty in the United States: 2017," U.S. Census Bureau, September 12, 2018. Note: The poverty level is defined as an income of $25,750 or below for a family of four according to Kimberly Amadeo, "Federal Poverty Level Guidelines and Chart," The Balance, January 22, 2019.

including 15 million children: National Center for Children in Poverty, "Child Poverty."

Little is being done to stop global climate change: Gary Langer, "Resources for the Future Poll: Public Attitudes on Global Warming," ABC News/ Stanford University, July 16, 2018.

5

Roughly two-thirds of Americans think: Pew Research Center, "The Public, the Political System and American Democracy," April 26, 2018.

"Never doubt that a small group of thoughtful, committed citizens": Donald Keys, *Earth at Omega: Passage to Planetization* (Wellesley, Mass.: Branden Publishing, 1978).

Chapter 1. You Can't Vote for President

7

"A ballot cast for President and Vice President of the United States": Monroe County Public Library, "Indiana Ballot November 2016," November 8, 2016.

9

Today, with twelve years of free, public education: Our World in Data, "Literacy," September 20, 2013.

Alexander Hamilton wrote that electors: Alexander Hamilton, "The Federalist Papers," Congress, March 12, 1788.

12

In forty-eight states and the District of Columbia: U.S. Electoral College, "Frequently Asked Questions."

In 2016, a study by National Public Radio found: Danielle Kurtzleben, "How to Win the Presidency with 23 Percent of the Popular Vote," NPR, November 2, 2016.

14

Four of the nine currently serving U.S. Supreme Court justices: Greg Price, "Brett Kavanaugh Will Be Fourth Supreme Court Justice Nominated by President Who Didn't Win the Popular Vote," *Newsweek,* October 6, 2018.

15

That means Wyoming, representing about half a million: World Population Review, "US States—Ranked by Population 2019."

Imagine you are one of the 53 million people: Mark O'Malley, "What Percentage of the US Population Lives in the Eastern, Central and Pacific Time Zones Respectively?," Quora.com, April 16, 2016.

16

In 2016, two-thirds of the campaign events: National Popular Vote, "Agreement Among the States to Elect the President by National Popular Vote."

17

"If you're one of the four out of every five Americans": Tim Alberta, "Is the Electoral College Doomed?," *Politico Magazine,* September/October 2017.

"It's kind of ridiculous": Peter Houston-Hencken, "Young Voters Seek the End of the Electoral College," *The Whitworthian,* November 10, 2016.

Maybe that is why voter turnout: Steve Silberstein, "How to Make the Electoral College Work for Everyone," *Washington Monthly,* March–May 2017.

18

"In addition, they are an effort to ensure": OAS, "Report to the Permanent Council1 OAS Electoral Observation Mission," January 17, 2017.

19

As Businessweek noted: Michael Waldman, "Majority Rule at Last: How to Dump the Electoral College without Changing the Constitution," *Washington Monthly,* April 2008.

Money flows unevenly, too: Andrew Reeves, "Political Disaster: Unilateral Powers, Electoral Incentives, and Presidential Disaster Declarations," *Journal of Politics* 73, no. 4 (2011): 1142-51.

Each presidential declaration brought: Andrew Reeves, "Political Disaster: Unilateral Powers, Electoral Incentives, and Presidential Disaster Declarations," *Journal of Politics* 73, no. 4 (2011): 1142-51.

According to statewide and Gallup polls: Christopher Pearson, "Agreement Among the States to Elect the President by National Popular Vote," State of Vermont House of Representatives, December 30, 2008.

20

The typical Electoral College map: 270 to Win, "2016 Presidential Election Results," July 20, 2017.

But more than 4 million Californians: Alex Padilla, California Secretary of State, "Historical Voter Registration Statistics," September 7, 2018.

But more than a third of Alabamans: "Alabama Results," *New York Times,* August 1, 2017.

"I had to run the entire state": T. J. Jerke, "Emmer Makes Push for Presidential Candidates to Invest Their Time in Smaller States," *West Central Tribune,* May 20, 2011.

21

This would likely create a much wider margin: Drew Desilver, "U.S. Trails Most Developed Countries in Voter Turnout," Pew Research Center, March 21, 2018.

22

"Electoral colleges are nowadays unknown": Matthew Shugart, email interviews, February 2019.

None have passed Congress: Tim Alberta, "Is the Electoral College Doomed?," *Politico Magazine,* September/October 2017.

"The current system is insane and unjustifiable": Tim Alberta, "Is the Electoral College Doomed?," *Politico Magazine,* September/October 2017. Note that Robert Bennett, a professor at Northwestern University School of Law, independently proposed a similar idea in his book *Taming the Electoral College.*

23

"We say the United States is ready for real democracy": Editorial staff, "States Join Forces Against Electoral College: A Piecemeal Approach May Be the Only Way to Kill the Anachronistic Institution," *Los Angeles Times,* June 5, 2006.

"A system that produces a majority": Editorial staff, "Time to Rethink Presidential Elections," *Denver Post,* April 18, 2006.

Have yours?: National Popular Vote, "Agreement Among the States to Elect the President by National Popular Vote," June 9, 2018.

24

"The State of _____ seeks to join": National Popular Vote, "The Agreement Among the States to Elect the President by National Popular Vote."

25

During debate over the measure in the Colorado Senate: National Popular Vote, "Status of National Popular Vote Bill in Each State: Colorado."

This Isn't a Democratic: National Popular Vote: "Status of National Popular Vote Bill in Each State: Illinois."

Organizations as diverse as the American Civil Liberties Union: Conservative Party of New York State, "Legislative Memo . . . in Support of the National Popular Vote," National Popular Vote.

Wisconsin electors adopted: George C. Edwards III, *Why the Electoral College Is Bad for America* (New Haven: Yale University Press, 2004).

29

"I do not recommend a Constitutional amendment lightly": Thomas E. Cronin, "The Direct Vote and the Electoral College: The Case for Meshing Things Up!," *Presidential Studies Quarterly* 9, no. 2 (1979): 144.

"[P]riority must be accorded to electoral college reform": Kurtis Lee, "In 1969, Democrats and Republicans United to Get Rid of the Electoral College. Here's What Happened," *Los Angeles Times,* December 19, 2016.

"A national popular vote means": Jeffrey Dinowitz, "Make New York Matter: Tell Albany to Pass the National Popular Vote," Huffington Post, June 28, 2010.

"Presidential elections should be a time": Joseph A. Griffo, "Griffo Says National Popular Vote Passage Could Become a Presidential Game Changer," National Popular Vote, June 7, 2010.

Chapter 2: Strange Maps

31

"I didn't want another holiday to be ruined by divisiveness": Tina Rosenberg, "Putting the Voters in Charge of Fair Voting," *New York Times,* January 23, 2018.

"Nobody trusted the system": Tina Rosenberg, "Putting the Voters in Charge of Fair Voting," *New York Times,* January 23, 2018.

32

The Salem Gazette published a political cartoon: Ari Berman, "Five Myths About Gerrymandering: No, GOP Dominance Isn't Just About 'Geography,'" *Washington Post,* March 8, 2018.

34

That number has been fixed by federal law: Tom Murse, "How Many Members Are in the House of Representatives?," Thought Co, September 10, 2018.

35

"A lot of people don't think about gerrymandering": Stateside staff, "Grassroots Movement Aims to Put New Redistricting Process on 2018 Ballot," Michigan Radio, February 27, 2017.

36

Compare these two voting district maps: Nate Cohn, Matthew Bloch, and Kevin Quealy, "The New Pennsylvania Congressional Map, District by District," *New York Times,* February 19, 2018.

"Democrats added a strange-looking": Matt Lewis, "Democrats Hate Gerrymandering—Except When They Get to Do It," Daily Beast, April 2, 2018.

37

"Partisan gerrymandering leads to dysfunction": NDRC, "NDRC Affiliate Invests in Michigan Redistricting Reform Effort," September 12, 2018.

"It has all the right mechanics of a board game": Kelly Norris, "H.S. Student Invents Game on Evils of Gerrymandering. Arnold Schwarzenegger Plays," NBC News, August 11, 2018.

Their marketing materials for the game: Kickstarter, Mapmaker: The Gerrymandering Game.

38

For years, many of the ten thousand students: Ballotpedia, "North Carolina's 12th Congressional District," 2018.

"This many students has the ability": Ella Nilsen, "North Carolina's Extreme Gerrymandering Could Save the House Republican Majority," Vox, May 8, 2018.

"I think that people in the state legislature are smart": Ella Nilsen, "North Carolina's Extreme Gerrymandering Could Save the House Republican Majority," Vox, May 8, 2018.

39

"I didn't need the help": Ari Berman, "How the GOP Is Resegregating the South," *The Nation,* January 31, 2012.

42

"If you have too high a percent African Americans in a House district": Kim Soffen, "How Racial Gerrymandering Deprives Black People of Political Power," *Washington Post* (blogs), June 9, 2016.

So four Democrats and nine Republicans: Christopher Ingraham, "America's Most Gerrymandered Congressional Districts: A Brief Overview of Crimes Against Geography in the 113th Congress," *Washington Post,* May 16, 2014.

When the Pennsylvania Supreme Court threw out: Nate Cohn, Matthew Bloch, and Kevin Quealy, "The New Pennsylvania Congressional Map, District by District," *New York Times,* February 19, 2018.

43

Instead, Republicans won thirty-three: Christopher Ingraham, "Here's the Completely Legal Way to 'Rig' an Election: Lawmakers Have Been at It for Decades," *Washington Post* (blogs), October 18, 2016.

44

He found that "over this period as a whole": Nicholas Stephanopoulos and Eric McGhee, "Partisan Gerrymandering and the Efficiency Gap," *University of Chicago Law School Chicago Unbound,* No. 493, 2014.

"It's easier than ever": Kevin Drum, "Computers Have Revolutionized Gerrymandering. The Supreme Court Should Take Notice," *Mother Jones,* February 26, 2017.

Not many other democracies in the world: Bernard Grofman and Lisa Handley, *Redistricting in Comparative Perspective,* Oxford University Press, August 15, 2008. Note: In the study of sixty counties, Handley found that in only fourteen do legislatures play a major role in redistricting. Twelve of those don't use our winner-takes-all approach, but rather give seats to runner-up parties. Only the United States and France allow legislative redistricting for districts where there is one winner no matter how split the vote.

"Today, most [districts] are simple": Andrew Prokop, "Gerrymandering, Explained," Vox, November 14, 2018.

45

Likewise, where Democrats drew the maps: Emily Bazelon, "The New Front in the Gerrymandering Wars: Democracy vs. Math," *New York Times,* August 29, 2017. Note that the gap between votes and seats is not wholly due to partisan bias. It's normal for the party with the majority of votes to get a bigger percentage of seats than of votes. The real problem is the partisan gerrymander, where one party will get a bigger bonus than the other, for the same vote percentage, according to UC Davis political scientist Matthew Shugart.

"I took one look at the map": Emily Bazelon, "The New Front in the Gerrymandering Wars: Democracy vs. Math," *New York Times,* August 29, 2017.

"Part of my intent was to create a map that": Ari Berman, "Five Myths About Gerrymandering: No, GOP Dominance Isn't Just About 'Geography,'" *Washington Post,* March 8, 2018.

A Republican state legislator: Matthew Rozsa, "Federal Court Rules Against North Carolina's Gerrymandered Map in Huge Win for Democrats," Salon, August 28, 2018.

"My side always took those bills": Ella Nilsen, "North Carolina's Extreme Gerrymandering Could Save the House Republican Majority," Vox, May 8, 2018.

46

In 2013, a Harris poll found that three-quarters of Republicans: Tina Rosenberg, "Putting the Voters in Charge of Fair Voting," *New York Times,* January 23, 2018.

Similar percentages of Democrats and independents: Cision, "Americans Across Party Lines Oppose Common Gerrymandering Practices," November 7, 2013.

"People instinctively get this": Tina Rosenberg, "Putting the Voters in Charge of Fair Voting," *New York Times,* January 23, 2018.

"What's really shocking": Abby Rapoport, "Does Gerrymandering Violate Free Speech?," *American Prospect,* January 30, 2012.

"When you're talking about the opportunity to turn your vote": Michael Wines, "'Pivotal Moment' in Politics as Gerrymandering Heads for Judgment Day," *New York Times,* April 22, 2017.

47

"Excessive partisanship": Chief Justice John Roberts, *Robert A. Rucho, et al. v. Common cause, et al.* (No. 18–422) and *Linda H. Lamone, et al. v. O. John Benisek,* et al. (No. 18–726). June 27, 2019.

"anti-democratic": Associate Justice Elena Kagan, *Robert A. Rucho, et al. v. Common cause, et al.* (No. 18–422) and *Linda H. Lamone, et al. v. O. John Benisek, et al.* (No. 18–726), June 27, 2019.

"Expect the abuse": Michael Wines, "Why the Supreme Court's Rulings Have Profound Implications for American Politics," *New York Times,* June 27, 2019.

48

"A lot of people understand that politicians": Erick Trickey, "A Grassroots Call to Ban Gerrymandering," *Atlantic Monthly,* September 23, 2018.

So she posted on Facebook: Tina Rosenberg, "Putting the Voters in Charge of Fair Voting," *New York Times,* January 23, 2018.

A study of voting maps conducted by the Brennan Center: Laura Royden and Michael Li, "Extreme Maps," Brennan Center for Justice at New York University School of Law, 2017.

49

Volunteers brought their clipboards: Tina Rosenberg, "Putting the Voters in Charge of Fair Voting," *New York Times,* January 23, 2018.

Fahey's mother: Editorial board, "Do-It-Yourself Legislative Redistricting," *New York Times,* July 21, 2018.

Li of the Brennan Center: Issie Lapowsky, "Midterm Voters Drew the Line on Gerrymandering," *Wired,* November 7, 2018.

50

Fahey herself expected her effort to fail: Stateside staff, "Grassroots Movement Aims to Put New Redistricting Process on 2018 Ballot," Michigan Radio, February 27, 2017.

"It was a lot of work": Stateside staff and Associated Press, "Redistricting Proposal Passes in Michigan," Michigan Radio, November 6, 2018.

51

"I'd go in, and they were looking tired": Tina Rosenberg, "Putting the Voters in Charge of Fair Voting," *New York Times,* January 23, 2018.

It's citizen work that makes all the difference: Stateside staff and Associated Press, "Redistricting Proposal Passes in Michigan," Michigan Radio, November 6, 2018.

53

For example, in Ohio, reformers got endorsements: Common Cause, "Redistricting Reform."

In September 2014, a group of citizens from Maryland: Jeff Guo, "Welcome to America's Most Gerrymandered District," *New Republic,* November 7, 2012.

54

Virginia, New York, and Massachusetts have all held competitions: Common Cause, "Redistricting Reform," and Emily Barasch, "The Twisted History of Gerrymandering in American Politics," *Atlantic Monthly,* September 19, 2012.

55

"It's time to terminate gerrymandering": Mas Greenwood, "Schwarzenegger: It's 'Time to Terminate Gerrymandering,'" The Hill, October 3, 2017.

"Partisan gerrymanders are incompatible": Mark Joseph Stern, "Notorious for a Reason," Slate, January 10, 2018.

"[Gerrymandering] is cancerous": Mary Bottari, "SCOTUS Prepares to Hear Case That Could Put an End to Hyper-Partisan Gerrymandering and One Party Rule," Huffington Post, September 15, 2017, citing the case *Benisek v. Lamone.*

"Americans deserve better": C-SPAN, "Congressman Earl Blumenauer on Redistricting and Gerrymandering," November 15, 2011.

Chapter 3: Unrepresentative Senate

57

"The gravest threat to fair representation": Jennifer McNulty, "Current Problems of U.S. Senate Rooted in History, Says Author," Newscenter, July 12, 2004.

Compare Wyoming's 574,000 people: U.S. Census Bureau, "2018 National and State Population Estimates," December 19, 2018.

"By 2040, 70 percent of Americans": Adam Wisnieski, "Next 100 Days: In the Era of Trump, NYS Is Out of Step and in the Crosshairs," CityLimits, June 30, 2017.

58

For example, the 29 million residents: World Population Review, "US States—Ranked by Population 2019."

"Every idea of proportion": Alexander Hamilton, "Federalist No. 22," Congress, December 14, 1787.

59

Nowadays, small states: Emily Badger, "As American as Apple Pie? The Rural Vote's Disproportionate Slice of Power," *New York Times,* November 21, 2016.

"From highway bills to homeland security": Adam Liptak, "Smaller States Find Outsize Clout Growing in Senate," *New York Times,* March 11, 2013.

The most recent example is Brett Kavanaugh: Parker Richards, "The People v. the U.S Senate," *Atlantic Monthly,* October 10, 2018.

60

"The filibuster allows lawmakers": Eric Levitz, "The Democrats' Irrational Love of the Filibuster Could Doom Their Agenda," *New York,* February 1, 2019.

"A Democracy Restoration Act": Burt Neuborne, "Divide States to Democratize the Senate," *Wall Street Journal,* November 19, 2018.

61

"These changes would make the Senate more": Matthew Shugart, email interview, February 2019.

"The filibuster is not in the Constitution": Chris Weigant, "The Third Nuclear Option: Ending the Legislative Filibuster," Huffington Post, March 31, 2017.

Chapter 4: Elections for Sale

63

Defeating it saved the company: Chisun Lee, Katherine Valde, Benjamin T. Brickner, and Douglas Keith, "Secret Spending in the States," Brennan Center for Justice at New York University School of Law, 2016.

64

But the donor who helped Tillis: Robert Maguire, "A New Low in Campaign Finance," *New York Times,* October 27, 2015.

In 2017, Doug Deason: Russ Choma, "Republicans Say They've Got to Act on Tax Reform—or Donors Might Get Mad," *Mother Jones,* November 10, 2017.

The vast majority of Americans: Arn Pearson, "GOP Wants to Flood Politics with Dark Money Using Hidden 'Policy Riders,'" Salon, March 20, 2018.

"The preferences of the average American": Martin Gilens and Benjamin Page, "Testing Theories of American Politics: Elites, Interest Groups, and Average Citizens," *Perspective on Politics* 12, no. 3 (2014): 564–81.

"The central point that emerges": Andrew Gumbel, "More Money More Political Problems," *Utne Reader,* July 2016.

66

Even though fewer than one in three Americans: Andy Kroll, "Is Citizens United to Blame for the Disastrous GOP Tax Bill?," *Mother Jones,* December 7, 2017.

"My donors are basically saying": Russ Choma, "Republicans Say They've Got to Act on Tax Reform—or Donors Might Get Mad," *Mother Jones,* November 10, 2017.

Norm Ornstein, a policy expert: Andy Kroll, "Is Citizens United to Blame for the Disastrous GOP Tax Bill?" *Mother Jones,* December 7, 2017.

67

Former Georgia Senator William Wyche Fowler: Andrew Gumbel, "More Money More Political Problems," *Utne Reader,* July 2016.

68

Four states (Missouri, Oregon, Utah, and Virginia): National Conference of State Legislatures, "Elections and Campaigns."

The 2016 presidential and congressional elections: Michael Beckel, "How Many Candidates Will Be Outgunned by Outside Groups in 2018?," Issue One, September 25, 2017.

71

The nonprofits can donate as much as they want: Kim Barker and Marian Wang, "Super-PACs and Dark Money: ProPublica's Guide to the New World of Campaign Finance," ProPublica, July 11, 2011.

"In my 33 years in Arizona politics": Chisun Lee, Katherine Valde, Benjamin T. Brickner, and Douglas Keith, "Secret Spending in the States," Brennan Center for Justice at New York University School of Law, 2016.

$5,000 to any political action committee per year: Federal Election Commission, "Understanding Ways to Support Federal Candidates."

72

"His image was distorted": James Bennet, "The New Price of American Politics," *Atlantic Monthly,* October 2012.

In 2018, one false ad: Kevin Roose, "We Asked for Examples of Election Misinformation. You Delivered," *New York Times,* November 4, 2018.

Another ad doctored a photo: Kevin Roose, "We Asked for Examples of Election Misinformation. You Delivered," *New York Times,* November 4, 2018.

Michael Sargeant of the Democratic Legislative Campaign Committee: Kim Barker, "How Dark Money Helped Democrats Hold a Key Senate Seat," *Atlantic Monthly,* December 27, 2012.

"For a relative pittance": Eliza Newlin Carney, "Report: Dark Money Surges in State and Local Elections," *American Prospect,* June 27, 2016.

73

State and local ballot measures: Chisun Lee, Katherine Valde, Benjamin T. Brickner, and Douglas Keith, "Secret Spending in the States," Brennan Center for Justice at New York University School of Law, 2016.

"Dark money is most likely": Chisun Lee, Katherine Valde, Benjamin T. Brickner, and Douglas Keith, "Secret Spending in the States," Brennan Center for Justice at New York University School of Law, 2016.

74

Seventy-eight percent of voters: End Citizens United, "Vulnerable and Compromised: Foreign Money Influencing U.S. Elections."

Trevor Potter, of the Campaign Legal Center: Russ Choma, "Mitch McConnell Just Made It Virtually Impossible to Police Dark Money in 2016," *Mother Jones,* December 17, 2015.

Fred Wertheimer, of the campaign reform group: Times Editorial Board, "The IRS Found a Way to Make 'Dark Money' Spent on Politics even Darker," *Los Angeles Times,* July 19, 2018.

One of the top donors to the American Petroleum Institute: End Citizens United, "Vulnerable and Compromised: Foreign Money Influencing U.S. Elections."

SABIC, a Saudi-owned chemical company: End Citizens United, "Vulnerable and Compromised: Foreign Money Influencing U.S. Elections," February 11, 2019; also see Lee Fang, "Loophole Allows Saudi Arabian Businesses to Spend Freely in Our Election," *The Nation,* October 11, 2012.

"Think of Burger King": Kathy Kiely, "Getting Illegal Foreign Money into US Campaigns? It's Easy, Experts Say," Moyers and Company, June 30, 2016.

75

In 2016, 11.4 million Americans: Ian Vandewalker and Lawrence Norden, "Getting Foreign Funds Out of America's Elections," Brennan Center for Justice at New York University School of Law, April 6, 2018.

A Russian state-controlled: Ian Vandewalker and Lawrence Norden, "Getting Foreign Funds Out of America's Elections," Brennan Center for Justice at New York University School of Law, April 6, 2018.

"Regardless of whether it affected the outcome": Ian Vandewalker and Lawrence Norden, "Getting Foreign Funds Out of America's Elections," Brennan Center for Justice at New York University School of Law, April 6, 2018.

76

It is also a constitutionally protected right of free speech: Cornell Law School, "First Amendment."

77

RepresentUs found that: RepresentUs, "The Problem," 2018.

78

"Can anybody guess how much": Farah Stockman, "For Voters Sick of Money in Politics, a New Pitch: No PAC Money Accepted," *New York Times,* August 12, 2018.

"Affluent Americans have substantially": DeNora Getachew and Ava Mehta, "Breaking Down Barriers: The Faces of Small Donor Public Financing," Brennan Center for Justice at New York University School of Law, June 9, 2016.

Another study showed: Andrew Gumbel, "More Money More Political Problems," *Utne Reader,* July 2016.

79

All the money in politics: Bob Biersack, "8 years later: How Citizens United Changed Campaign Finance," Open Secrets, February 7, 2018.

To win a Senate seat: RepresentUs, "The Problem," 2018.

80

"Historically, for school board races": Chisun Lee, Katherine Valde, Benjamin T. Brickner, and Douglas Keith, "Secret Spending in the States," Brennan Center for Justice at New York University School of Law, 2016.

An Oklahoma State University study found: Sean McElwee, "Why Voting Matters," Demos, September 16, 2015.

Members of Congress: Celestine Bohlen, "American Democracy Is Drowning in Money," *New York Times,* September 20, 2017.

82

Beto O'Rourke (D) raised $79 million: Open Secrets, "Beto O'Rourke," 2017–2018.

"It's a major theme of the campaign": Farah Stockman, "For Voters Sick of Money in Politics, a New Pitch: No PAC Money Accepted," *New York Times,* August 12, 2018.

Fifty-two members: Karl Evers-Hillstrom, "Democrats Are Rejecting Corporate PACs: Does It Mean Anything?," Open Secrets, December 7, 2018.

Several presidential hopefuls for the 2020 election: Elizabeth Gurdus, "Cory Booker Joins Kirsten Gillibrand and Other Senate Democrats in Rejecting Corporate PAC Donations," CNBC, February 14, 2018.

"We need to get rid of": Farah Stockman, "For Voters Sick of Money in Politics, a New Pitch: No PAC Money Accepted," *New York Times,* August 12, 2018.

In fact, three-quarters of voters: Bradley Jones, "Most Americans Want to Limit Campaign Spending, Say Big Donors Have Greater Political Influence," Pew Research Center, May 8, 2018.

83

Regarding those nonprofit: Eliza Newlin Carney, "Fighting over Secret Money," *American Prospect,* June 27, 2016.

"No doubt it is ridiculously difficult": Lawrence Lessig, "The Only Realistic Way to Fix Campaign Finance," *New York Times,* July 21, 2015.

The Citizens United *ruling stated:* Patt Morrison, "'Dark money' Is Smashing Our System of Political Openness. How One State Is Fighting Back—and Winning," *Los Angeles Times,* August 1, 2018.

In 2018, forty-two states: National Conference of State Legislatures, "Elections and Campaigns."

84

The United States currently has twenty-seven: Juhem Navarro-Rivera and Emmanuel Caicedo, "Public Funding for Electoral Campaigns," Demos, July 28, 2017.

Fourteen of these programs: National Conference of State Legislatures, "Overview of State Laws on Public Financing," 2018.

New York City's eight-to-one match: New York City Campaign Finance Board, "Join the Matching Funds Program."

"The promise of the vouchers": Russell Berman, "How Can the U.S. Shrink the Influence of Money in Politics?," *Atlantic Monthly,* March 16, 2016.

85

Public financing widens: Mimi Murray Digby Marziani and Adam Skaggs, "More than Combating Corruption: The Other Benefits of Public Financing," Brennan Center for Justice at New York University School of Law, October 7, 2011.

But when they heard that a $5 donation: Mimi Murray Digby Marziani and Adam Skaggs, "More than Combating Corruption: The Other Benefits of Public Financing," Brennan Center for Justice at New York University School of Law, October 7, 2011.

Publicly financed elections have allowed: Mimi Murray Digby Marziani and Adam Skaggs, "More than Combating Corruption: The Other Benefits of Public Financing," Brennan Center for Justice at New York University School of Law, October 7, 2011.

The Center for Governmental Studies found: Mimi Murray Digby Marziani and Adam Skaggs, "More than Combating Corruption: The Other Benefits of Public Financing," Brennan Center for Justice at New York University School of Law, October 7, 2011.

"I didn't come from money": DeNora Getachew and Ava Mehta, "Breaking Down Barriers: The Faces of Small Donor Public Financing," Brennan Center for Justice at New York University School of Law, 2016.

Andrew Hall, professor of political science: Matthew Sheffield, "Could Public Funding of Elections Revolutionize Politics?," Salon, February 20, 2018.

86

Such programs also tend to shift: Public Campaign, "Small Donor Solutions for Big Money: The 2014 Elections and Beyond," November 21, 2014.

Janet Napolitano (D): Mimi Murray Digby Marziani and Adam Skaggs, "More than Combating Corruption: The Other Benefits of Public Financing," Brennan Center for Justice at New York University School of Law, October 7, 2011.

One study found that: Peter L. Francia and Paul S. Herrnson, "The Impact of Public Finance Laws on Fundraising in State Legislative Elections," *American Politics Research* 31, no. 5 (September 1, 2003): 520–39.

"[The program] has made me": Public Campaign, "Small Donor Solutions for Big Money: The 2014 Elections and Beyond," November 21, 2014.

Public funding for campaigns: Public Campaign, "Small Donor Solutions for Big Money: The 2014 Elections and Beyond," November 21, 2014.

The programs are popular: Adam Smith, "Poll: Voters Think Congress Cares More About Donors than Them," Every Voice, November 10, 2014.

87

And New Yorkers strengthened: Hazel Millard, "Another Election Winner—Public Financing," Brennan Center for Justice at New York University School of Law, November 12, 2018.

The price tag of U.S. elections dwarfs: Nick Thompson, "International Campaign Finance: How Do Countries Compare?," CNN, March 5, 2012.

Some countries ban political ads: Paul Waldman, "How Our Campaign Finance System Compares to Other Countries," *American Prospect,* April 4, 2014.

"The lack of spending limits": Paul Waldman, "How Our Campaign Finance System Compares to Other Countries," *American Prospect,* April 4, 2014.

Elections in other parts of the world: Nick Thompson, "International Campaign Finance: How Do Countries Compare?," CNN, March 5, 2012.

88

"The bottom line is": Marilyn W. Thompson, "The Price of Public Money," *Atlantic Monthly,* May 27, 2016.

In 2008, Barack Obama: Marilyn W. Thompson, "The Price of Public Money," *Atlantic Monthly,* May 27, 2016.

89

"It's not just a matter of exhorting": Marilyn W. Thompson, "The Price of Public Money," *Atlantic Monthly,* May 27, 2016.

For example, Bernie Sanders's 2016: Susie Poppick, "What's Your Campaign Donation Really Worth?," CNBC, March 31, 2016.

The U.S. Supreme Court has ruled: Austin Graham, "Innovative Public Financing System Has Broadened Political Engagement for Seattle Residents," CLC, September 22, 2017.

90

"I feel strongly that our voices": Ellen Moorhouse, "Member Spotlight: Ellen Chaffee and Dina Butcher, North Dakota," RepresentUs, July 30, 2018.

93

"Campaign finance is like the gateway issue": Nina Heyn, "Food for the Soul: Dark Money," *Solari Report,* August 15, 2018.

"Virtually everybody in the Senate": Arn Pearson, "GOP Wants to Flood Politics with Dark Money Using Hidden 'Policy Riders,'" Salon, March 20, 2018.

"Money's dominance over politics": Wolf Pac, "The Problem: The United States Government Is No Longer Accountable to the People."

"If we build a new system that makes everyday Americans": Every Voice, "Our Plan," 2018.

Chapter 5: The Right to Lie

95

In the 2016 presidential campaign, PolitiFact: Jack Myers, "The Truth About Lying in Political Advertising," Huffington Post, November 15, 2016.

Stacey Abrams (D): Eugene Kiely, D'Angelo Gore, and Robert Farley, "Republican Closing Ads: Immigration," Fact Check, November 2, 2018.

Illinois state senate candidate Barrett Davie (R): Kristen McQueary, "Commentary: Campaign Ads and Whoppers," *Chicago Tribune,* October 23, 2018.

"The theory is that government punishment": I-Hsien Sherwood, "Truthiness in Advertising: Why Trump Gets to Lie but You Don't," Campaign US, March 8, 2016.

96

Journalists and fact checkers try: David Schultz, "Is There a First Amendment Right to Lie in Politics?," Cleveland.com, July 5, 2014.

it applies the same standards no matter where an ad appears: Federal Trade Commission, "Truth in Advertising."

97

When Kellogg falsely claimed: Jayson DeMers, "6 False Advertising Scandals You Can Learn From," *Entrepreneur,* June 6, 2018. Federal Trade Commission, "FTC Investigation of Ad Claims that Rice Krispies Benefits Children's Immunity Leads to Stronger Order Against Kellogg," Press release on FTC Docket No. C-4262, June 3, 2010.

for related lawsuits: Manatt Phelps & Phillips LLP, "Kellogg settles again, this time over Rice Krispies," Lexology.com, January 31, 2011.

When the ride-share app Uber: I-Hsien Sherwood, "Truthiness in Advertising: Why Trump Gets to Lie but You Don't," Campaign US, March 8, 2016. William Hoffman, "Uber Settles Lawsuit over Misleading 'Safest Ride on the Road' Ads," Inverse.com, April 16, 2016.

And Red Bull's unproven claim: Jayson DeMers, "6 False Advertising Scandals You Can Learn From," *Entrepreneur,* June 6, 2018. James Hamblin, "Red Bull is just Soda," *The Atlantic,* October 9, 2014.

"You hear people say": Amy Sullivan, "Truth in Advertising? Not for Political Ads," *Time,* September 23, 2008.

98

"A good argument can be made": David Schultz, "The Constitution Should Not Protect a Right to Lie in Politics," Minnpost, October 18, 2018.

"Prohibiting lying actually enhances": David Schultz, "The Constitution Should Not Protect a Right to Lie in Politics," Minnpost, October 18, 2018.

A poll conducted by the Association of Young Americans: Kenneth Terrell, "AARP Poll: Honesty in Government Matters Most Across Generations," AARP, October 16, 2018.

Chapter 6: Suppressing the Vote

101

For missing that election: Chiraag Bains, "You Have the Right to Vote. Use It or Lose It, the Supreme Court Says," *Washington Post,* June 13, 2018.

"Few of us have cars": Paula Span, "Older Voters Stymied by Tighter ID Requirements," *New York Times,* November 24, 2017.

102

"You're going to put money": Wendy R. Weiser, "Voter Suppression: How Bad? (Pretty Bad)," *American Prospect*, October 1, 2014.

So she was shocked to receive a letter: Siddhartha Mahanta, "The GOP's War on Voting Comes to Washington," *Mother Jones,* December 1, 2011.

103

To Sharp, voting is: Dan Harris and Melia Patria, "Is True the Vote Intimidating Minority Voters from Going to the Polls?," ABC News, November 2, 2012.

For instance, the Interstate Crosscheck System: Dale Ho, "Trump's Voter Suppression Efforts Have Begun," *New York Times,* July 3, 2017.

There's little evidence of people with two registrations: John Kowal, Brennan Center for Justice, email interview, February 2019.

104

Sharp traveled to the Board of Elections: Siddhartha Mahanta, "The GOP's War on Voting Comes to Washington," *Mother Jones,* December 1, 2011.

While keeping the voter rolls accurate: Siddhartha Mahanta, "The GOP's War on Voting Comes to Washington," *Mother Jones,* December 1, 2011.

"We found that between 2014 and 2016": Jonathan Brater, Kevin Morris, Myrna Pérez, and Christopher Deluzio, "Purges: A Growing Threat to the Right to Vote," Brennan Center for Justice at New York University School of Law, July 20, 2018.

From 2013 to 2018, roughly a thousand polling places: Matt Vasilogambros, "Polling Places Remain a Target Ahead of November Elections," The Pew Trusts, September 4, 2018.

105

In 2018, the thirteen thousand registered voters: Statistical Atlas, "Race and Ethnicity in Dodge City, Kansas."

Election officials had moved their one polling place: Associated Press, "Early Voting Ahead of Midterms Reveals Vote-Related Problems," *The Columbian,* November 2, 2018.

Having to vote in an unfamiliar voting place: Matt Vasilogambros, "Polling Places Remain a Target Ahead of November Elections," The Pew Trusts, September 4, 2018.

"You can basically lessen the turnout": Matt Vasilogambros, "Polling Places Remain a Target Ahead of November Elections," The Pew Trusts, September 4, 2018.

"This is not just an issue of fairness": Matt Vasilogambros, "Polling Places Remain a Target Ahead of November Elections," The Pew Trusts, September 4, 2018.

106

In the 2012 presidential election: Wendy R. Weiser, "Voter Suppression: How Bad? (Pretty Bad)," *American Prospect,* October 1, 2014.

Wisconsin cut early voting: Ari Berman and Pema Levy, "Rigged," *Mother Jones,* November/December 2017.

"If I'm not eating or sleeping": Danny Hakim and Michael Wines, "'They Don't Really Want Us to Vote': How Republicans Made It Harder," *New York Times,* November 3, 2018.

After Florida cut a week of early voting: Ari Berman and Pema Levy, "Rigged," *Mother Jones,* November/December 2017.

Roughly one in five waited in line: Charles Stewart III, "2016 Survey of the Performance of American Elections Final Report," Legends Vote, 2016.

107

In 2013, when the state instituted: Maya Rhodan, "ID Laws Present Problems for Women and Trans Voters in Texas," Time.com, October 24, 2013.

108

"We have hard evidence": Ari Berman and Pema Levy, "Rigged," *Mother Jones,* November/December 2017.

109

No other democracy: Frederic Charles Schaffer and Tova Andrea Wang, "Is Everyone Else Doing It? Indiana's Voter Identification Law in International Perspective," *Harvard Law & Policy Review* 3, Summer 2009.

One study out of Harvard: Charles Ogletree, "'Free' voter IDs are costly, Harvard Law report finds," Harvard Law Today, June 26, 2014.

These voter ID costs are much high than that: Catherine Rampell, "Catherine Rampell: Voter Suppression Laws Are Already Deciding Elections," *Washington Post,* November 11, 2014, and Oyez, "Harper v. Virginia Board of Elections," January 26, 1966.

110

"There is scant evidence": Selby W. Gardner, "Barack Obama, in Austin, Says U.S. Only 'Advanced Democracy' That Makes Voting Harder," Politifact, June 20, 2016.

But these cases are easily caught: Kira Zalan, "The 'Myth' of Polling Place Fraud," *U.S. News,* April 24, 2012.

The number of successful prosecutions: Kira Zalan, "The 'Myth' of Polling Place Fraud," *U.S. News,* April 24, 2012.

Consider the work of the U.S. Justice Department: Siddhartha Mahanta, "The GOP's War on Voting Comes to Washington," *Mother Jones,* December 1, 2011.

In Pennsylvania, the government admitted: Viviette Applewhite et al., "In the Commonwealth Court of Pennsylvania," Moritz College of Law, June 17, 2013.

"leaders concede that there has never been a case": Frederic Charles Schaffer and Tova Andrea Wang, "Is Everyone Else Doing It? Indiana's Voter Identification Law in International Perspective," *Harvard Law & Policy Review* 3, Summer 2009.

111

Election officials in North Carolina: Stephanie Saul, "Looking, Very Closely, for Voter Fraud," *New York Times,* September 17, 2012.

"It makes no sense for individual voters": Siddhartha Mahanta, "The GOP's War on Voting Comes to Washington," *Mother Jones,* December 1, 2011.

112

13 cases of in-person voter: Dave Gilson, Jaeah Lee, and Hamed Aleaziz, "UFO Sightings Are More Common Than Voter Fraud," *Mother Jones,* July/August 2012.

And P.O. Boxes that they used: Ashoka Mukpo, "Supreme Court Enables Mass Disenfranchisement of North Dakota's Native Americans," ACLU, October 12, 2018. Also see Ruth Bader Ginsburg's dissent No. 18a335.

113

Ten percent of citizens with disabilities: Rabia Belt, "Contemporary Voting Rights Controversies Through the Lens of Disability," *Stanford Law Review* 68, no. 6 (June 2016): 1491–1550.

Eighteen percent of people over the age of sixty-five: Siddhartha Mahanta, "The GOP's War on Voting Comes to Washington," *Mother Jones,* December 1, 2011.

In 1979, the U.S. Supreme Court: Justia, *"Symm v. United States,"* 1979.

Pennsylvania requires student IDs: Campus Vote Project, "College Students and Voting: A Campus Vote Project Perspective."

114

"What I used for voter registration": Maya Rhodan, "ID Laws Present Problems for Women and Trans Voters in Texas," Time.com, October 24, 2013.

"Because many women change their last name": Maya Rhodan, "ID Laws Present Problems for Women and Trans Voters in Texas," Time.com, October 24, 2013.

That's almost 43 million: Calculated from "Resident Population of the United States by Sex and Age as of July 1, 2017 (in Millions)," Statista.com.

115

Ari Berman, author of Give Us the Ballot: Mary Claire Blakeman, "Anti-voter laws worse than Russian meddling," *Louisiana Weekly,* June 19, 2017.

Eight percent of voting-age: Jessica Gonzalez, "New State Voting Laws: A Barrier to the Latino Vote?," Congressional Hispanic Caucus Institute White Paper, April 15, 2012.

116

a staggering 25 percent of black people: Kevin Drum, "The Dog That Voted and Other Election Fraud Yarns," *Mother Jones,* July/August 2012.

Researchers at the University of California, San Diego: Vann Newkirk II, "How Voter ID Laws Discriminate," *Atlantic Monthly,* February 18, 2017.

"before enacting the law": Carol Anderson, *One Person, No Vote* (New York: Bloomsbury, 2018).

Stewart estimates that in the November 2016 election: Ari Berman and Pema Levy, "Rigged," *Mother Jones,* November/December 2017.

117

"By instituting strict voter ID laws": Vann Newkirk II, "How Voter ID Laws Discriminate," *Atlantic Monthly,* February 18, 2017.

119

"I'm disappointed in my government": Ari Berman and Pema Levy, "Rigged," *Mother Jones,* November/December 2017.

Thirty-four states offer some early voting: Ballotpedia, "Early Voting," January 30, 2018.

120

Vassar College political groups: Campus Vote Project, "College Students and Voting: A Campus Vote Project Perspective."

121

"Repeated investigations show": Richard North Patterson, "The Very Real Threat of Voter Suppression," *Boston Globe,* November 21, 2017.

"Voters shouldn't lose their right": Sean Sullivan and Sari Horwitz, "Federal Court Rules Against Ohio's Purges of Voter Rolls," *Washington Post,* September 24, 2016.

"Republicans should be less afraid": Ari Berman, "How the GOP Candidates Are Blocking the Vote," *The Nation,* January 28, 2016.

"We have to demand attention": Mary Claire Blakeman, "Anti-voter Laws Worse than Russian Meddling," *Louisiana Weekly,* June 19, 2017.

Chapter 7: Shut Out of Statehood

123

From the time Washington, D.C.: Tessa Berenson, "Here's Why Washington D.C. Isn't a State," *Time,* April 15, 2016.

D.C. residents pay the second-highest: Richard Barrington, "Which States Pay the Most Federal Taxes," Money Rates, April 3, 2018.

Roughly two thousand D.C. citizens: Statehood DC, "DC Statehood."

That's a larger population: World Population Review, "US States—Ranked by Population 2019."

Puerto Ricans living on the island: Rebecca Pilar Buckwalker-Poza, "The 52-State Strategy: The Case for Puerto Rico," *Washington Monthly,* July/August 2018.

124

"We want to be treated like any other state": Story Hinckley, "Should Washington, D.C. Become the 51st State? Why Sanders and Clinton Say Yes," *Christian Science Monitor,* June 13, 2016.

A recent estimate puts Puerto Rico: Jo Craven McGinty, "Statehood for Puerto Ricans: Billions More in U.S. Programs—and in Taxes," *Wall Street Journal,* November 4, 2017.

Both improved economically: Olga Khazan, "Why Does Puerto Rico Want Statehood, Anyway?," *Washington Post,* December 26, 2012.

Part of the problem: Alexia Fernández Campbell, "Puerto Rico's Push for Statehood, Explained," Vox, September 24, 2018.

125

Some Puerto Ricans want to remain separate: CBS News, "Puerto Rican Voters Overwhelmingly Chose Statehood, Governor Says," June 11, 2017.

Almost half said they want Puerto Rico: Alexia Fernández Campbell, "Puerto Rico's Push for Statehood, Explained," Vox, September 24, 2018.

Governor Rosselló also wrote a formal letter: Alexia Fernández Campbell, "Puerto Rico's Push for Statehood, Explained," Vox, September 24, 2018.

126

"I'm pleased to be one of the sponsors": Nicole Acevedo, "New Bipartisan Bill Calls for Puerto Rico Statehood," June 27, 2018.

Part of the lack of movement: Kyle Dropp and Brendan Nyhan, "Nearly Half of Americans Don't Know Puerto Ricans Are Fellow Citizens," *New York Times,* September 26, 2017.

"[Congress] will just put off a decision": Gregory Scruggs, "Could Hurricane Maria Force a Change in Puerto Rico's Relationship to the U.S.?," *Americas Quarterly,* October 4, 2017.

127

The United States has other territories: Puerto Rico Report, "Puerto Rico Is Not a State: Why Not?," October 20, 2017.

Nearly half favor statehood: Rebecca Pilar Buckwalker-Poza, "The 52-State Strategy: The Case for Puerto Rico," *Washington Monthly,* July/August 2018.

Both Democrats and Republicans have expressed: Richard Fausset, "In Puerto Rico, Fiscal Crisis Renews Statehood Debate," *New York Times,* May 17, 2017.

The D.C. Republican Party backs D.C. statehood: PR51st, "Democratic and Republican Party Platforms on Puerto Rican Statehood."

Senator Bernie Sanders (I) thinks: Story Hinckley, "Should Washington, D.C. Become the 51st State? Why Sanders and Clinton Say Yes," *Christian Science Monitor,* June 13, 2016.

While being awarded statehood: Robert Longley, "How the US Statehood Process Works," Thought Co, October 17, 2018.

Chapter 8: Barred from Voting

132

"To be shut out of the democratic process": Beth Reinhard, "States Ease Restrictions on Voting by Felons," *Wall Street Journal,* March 5, 2017.

133

Fourteen states and: National Conference of State Legislatures, "Felon Voting Rights," December 21, 2018.

134

But many bar voting: Drug Treatment, "Marijuana Felony Possession Amounts."

In Mississippi, if you pay $100 for something: "Summary of State Bad Check Laws," *American Lawyers Quarterly,* January 2007.

136

In fact, we have the highest incarceration rate: World Prison Brief, "Highest to Lowest—Prison Population Rate."

Also, no other democracy in the world strips citizens: Christopher Uggen and Jeff Manza, "Democratic Contraction? Political Consequences of Felon Disenfranchisement in the United States," *American Sociological Review* 67, no. 6 (2002): 777–803.

Twenty-one countries, including Austria: ProCon, "International Comparison of Felon Voting Laws," April 11, 2018.

138

Telling a park ranger you cleaned your site: Laura Dimon, "8 Ways We Regularly Commit Felonies Without Realizing It," Mic.com, April 3, 2014.

Violating a website's terms of use: Jon Rosenberg, "7 Felonies You've Probably Committed in Your Lifetime," Maxim.com, May 16, 2013.

In fact, half of federal prison inmates: Sam Taxy, Julie Samuels, and William Adams, "Drug Offenders in Federal Prison: Estimates of Characteristics Based on Linked Data," Department of Justice, October 2015.

Even the most upstanding citizens: Harvey Silverglate, *Three Felonies a Day* (New York: Encounter Books, 2011).

139

"I thought I was practicing my right": Jack Healy, "Penalty: Up to 2 Years in Prison. Charge: Casting an Illegal Vote," *New York Times,* August 5, 2018.

In 2017, only eleven people were convicted: Jack Healy, "Penalty: Up to 2 Years in Prison. Charge: Casting an Illegal Vote," *New York Times,* August 5, 2018.

140

When the downsides of voting illegally: Farah Stockman, "After Serving Their Time, Fighting to Get Out the Vote," *New York Times,* May 16, 2013.

141

It's one in five in Kentucky: Christopher Uggen, Ryan Larson, and Sarach Shannon, "6 Million Lost Voters," The Sentencing Project, October 6, 2016.

Something is going on: Kim Farbota, "Black Crime Rates: What Happens When Numbers Aren't Neutral," Huffington Post, September 2, 2015.

Once convicted, black people get longer sentences: German Lopez, "Everyone Does Drugs, but Only Minorities Are Punished for It," Vox, July 1, 2014.

142

A Virginia state senator was quoted: Sheryl Gay Stolberg and Erik Eckholm, "Virginia Governor Restores Voting Rights to Felons," *New York Times,* April 22, 2016.

In Mississippi, politicians called for disenfranchisement: Marc Mauer and Meda Chesney-Lind, *Invisible Punishment: The Collateral Consequences of Mass Imprisonment* (New York: New Press, 2003).

As a result, you could lose your vote: "Free the Vote," NAACP Legal Defense and Educational Fund and The Sentencing Project.

Likewise, in Alabama: Andrew L. Shapiro, "Challenging Criminal Disenfranchisement Under the Voting Rights Act: A New Strategy," *Yale Law Journal* 103, no. 2 (1993): 537–66.

"The original intent was to keep freed slaves": Gaby Del Valle, "Felon Couldn't Vote for His Wife, So He's Pushing to Change the Law," Daily Beast, April 28, 2017.

143

In practice, more than four hundred thousand: "Free the Vote," NAACP Legal Defense and Educational Fund and The Sentencing Project.

Studies show that candidates are less likely: Fox Butterfield, "2 Studies Find Laws on Felons Forbid Many Black Men to Vote," *New York Times,* September 23, 2004.

145

"I'd like to set a good example": Sentencing Project, "Marlo Hargrove and David Waller."

Research suggests voters are more likely: Nonprofit Vote, "Benefits for Voters."

"voting appears to be part of a package": Christopher Uggen, Clem Brooks, and Jeff Manza, "Public Attitudes Towards Felon Disenfranchisement in the United States," *American Association for Public Opinion Research* 68, no. 2 (2004): 275–86.

In its policy statement: American Correctional Association, "Public Correctional Policy on Restoration of Voting Rights for Felony Offenders, No. 2005-3," Public Correctional Policies, January 25, 2017.

146

Nearly two-thirds would extend the right: Christopher Uggen, Clem Brooks, and Jeff Manza, "Public Attitudes Towards Felon Disenfranchisement in the United States," *American Association for Public Opinion Research* 68, no. 2 (2004): 275–86.

147

"WHEREAS, the loss of the right to vote": American Probation and Parole Association, "Resolution Supporting Restoration of Voting Rights Released," Brennan Center for Justice at New York University School of Law, October 17, 2007.

"Nowhere in the U.S. Constitution": Kira Lerner, "This Man Can't Vote Today Because Kentucky's GOP Governor Reversed a Major Voting Rights Victory," Think Progress, May 17, 2016.

148

"Every citizen of the United States": Michael Lind, "Voting Is Not a Right," Salon, May 23, 2013.

149

"The last thing we want to do": Jane C. Timm, "Most States Disenfranchise Felons. Maine and Vermont Allow Inmates to Vote from Prison," NBC News, February 26, 2018.

"I look at it like": Susan Sharon, "Prison Inmates Can Vote in Maine, and Interest This Year Has Been High," *Bangor Daily News,* November 4, 2016.

Members of Congress: Benjamin L. Cardin, "S.1588—Democracy Restoration Act of 2017," Congress.gov, July 19, 2017.

"The right of an individual who is a citizen": Benjamin L. Cardin, "S.1588—Democracy Restoration Act of 2017," Congress.gov, July 19, 2017.

150

A New York governor: Sentencing Project, "Disenfranchisement News: Felony Disenfranchisement and the Midterm Elections," October 18, 2018.

A federal judge called the Florida system: Jon Kamp, "Judge Rules Against Florida's Felon Voting Rights Restoration Process," *Wall Street Journal,* February 2, 2018.

In November 2018, 64 percent of Florida voters: Langston Taylor, "Most Ex-felons Can Register to Vote Tuesday if All Terms of Their Sentence Are Met," *Miami Herald,* January 4, 2019.

"There were a lot of tears": Langston Taylor, "Most Ex-felons Can Register to Vote Tuesday if All Terms of Their Sentence Are Met," *Miami Herald,* January 4, 2019.

151

"This is an entirely new voting bloc": Farah Stockman, "After Serving Their Time, Fighting to Get Out the Vote," *New York Times,* May 13, 2018.

"As I ran my pen": Right to Vote Project, "My First Vote," Brennan Center for Justice at New York University School of Law, July 5, 2009.

153

"The right to vote is a sacred one": Tal Kopan, "Paul Takes Voter Rights Fight Home," *Politico Magazine,* February 19, 2014.

"People have served their time": Sheryl Gay Stolberg and Erik Eckholm, "Virginia Governor Restores Voting Rights to Felons," *New York Times,* April 22, 2016.

"I was asked . . . about felon disenfranchisement": Charlie Crist, "Charlie Crist: Ex-felons in Florida Need Their Voting Rights Back," *USA Today,* February 11, 2018.

"The United States may have the most restrictive": John Conyers, "Felon Voting," ProCon, March 16, 2016.

Chapter 9: Too Young to Vote?

155

"I think it's important that we all do our part": Takoma Park City TV, "16 Year Old Votes!," November 1, 2013.

156

People told her: National Youth Rights Association, "An Interview with the Voting Age Activists of Greenbelt, Md.," December 7, 2017.

"If you explain the reasoning": Ema Smith, "How Young People Pushed Greenbelt, Maryland, to Lower the City's Voting Age," *Teen Vogue,* November 22, 2017.

160

Lowering the voting age: Aaron C. Davis, "16-Year-Olds in D.C. Could Vote for President in 2016, Under Proposal," *Washington Post,* November 3, 2015.

Almost 16 million young people: Corporation for National and Community Service, "Issue Brief: Youth Helping America," November 2005.

161

For instance, millions of young people: Chris Hedges, "Translating America For Parents and Family; Children of Immigrants Assume Difficult Roles," *New York Times,* June 19, 2000.

On any given day: Jocelyn S. Wikle, Alexander C. Jensen, and Alexander M. Hoagland, "Adolescent Caretaking of Younger Siblings," *Social Science Research* 71 (March 2018): 72–84.

163

"From a public official's point of view": Joe Heim, "D.C.'s 16- and 17-Year-Olds Are Eager to Vote for President. But Should They?," *Washington Post,* November 3, 2015.

165

Assessments out of Rutgers University: AAPSS, "Daniel Hart: Time for American Teens Under 18 to Hit the Polls," February 23, 2011.

"If you look at the kind of preparation": AAPSS, "Daniel Hart: Time for American Teens Under 18 to Hit the Polls," February 23, 2011.

166

"It's time for us to stand up": "State of the Union," CNN, February 18, 2018.

"My parents tell me 'don't resist'": Alli Maloney, "These 2 Columbus Teens Are Rallying Against Trump's Muslim Ban," *Teen Vogue,* February 4, 2017.

James Jelin, sixteen, a junior: Jen Lynds, "MSSM Student to Testify on Child-Support Bill He Originated," *Bangor Daily News,* February 12, 2011.

Teenager Diego Morris of Phoenix: Ty Brennan, "Valley Teen Testifies in Front of Congress," Fox10, February 29, 2016.

167

"You know, lots of people ask me": John Bowden, "Teen Candidate for Kansas Governor Says He's Campaigning Against 'Old Man Principles,'" *The Hill,* March 3, 2018.

168

"They don't want to just protest": Kara Voght, "There's a Growing Movement to Let 16-Year-Olds Vote. It Would Change Everything," *Mother Jones,* April 3, 2018.

"I'm forming my own political views": Elena Schneiderjan, "Students in Maryland Test Civic Participation and Win Right to Vote," *New York Times,* September 9, 2015.

169

Maybe that's why roughly half of millennials: Pew Research Center, "Millennials in Adulthood," March 7, 2014.

170

Only about 40 percent of those eligible voters: United States Elections Project, "Voter Turnout Demographics."

171

"It could be that 18": Jennifer Levine, "Teen Spirit Spurs Bill to Lower Voting Age," *Wall Street Journal,* July 18, 2012.

Young adults who lived at home: Yosef Bhatti and Kasper M. Hansen, "Leaving the Nest and the Social Act of Voting: Turnout Among First-Time Voters," *Elections, Public Opinion and Parties* 22, no. 4 (2012): 380–406.

People who vote in one election: Alan S. Gerber, Donald P. Green, and Ron Shachar, "Voting May Be Habit Forming: Evidence from a Randomized Field Experiment," Institute for Social and Policy Studies at Yale University, 2003, and Zachary Crockett, "The Case for Allowing 16-Year-Olds to Vote," Vox, November 7, 2016.

Sixteen-year-old Theo Shoag: Joe Heim, "D.C.'s 16- and 17-Year-Olds Are Eager to Vote for President. But Should They?," *Washington Post,* November 3, 2015.

173

When the town council in Hyattsville, Maryland: Arelis Hernandez, "Hyattsville Lawmakers Lower Voting Age to 16," *Washington Post,* January 8, 2015.

174

"More than half of all the San Francisco": Zachary Crockett, "The Case for Allowing 16-Year-Olds to Vote," Vox, November 7, 2016.

Advocate Lorelie Vaisse says: Zachary Crockett, "The Case for Allowing 16-Year-Olds to Vote," Vox, November 7, 2016.

"Young people are truly interested": Vote16 SF, "Historic Measure Almost Passes: More than 172,000 Vote to Extend Voting Rights to 16-Year-Olds for Municipal Elections," November 28, 2016.

177

"Our country was founded": Devon Miller, "'Millennial' Legislators Bill Aims to Lower Voting Age in California," Hometownstation.com, March 10, 2017.

"Teens between 14 and 18": Laurence Tribe (@tribelaw), "Teens between 14 and 18 have far better BS detectors, on average, than 'adults' 18 and older. Wouldn't it be great if the voting age were lowered to 16? Just a pipe dream, I know, but . . . #Children'sCrusade?," Twitter, February 19, 2018.

"I got to vote in 1972": Zaid Jilani, "Despite Surging Youth Activism, Members of Congress Are Reluctant to Lower the Voting Age," *The Intercept,* March 13, 2018.

"We're all in this community together": Devyn Rafols-Nuñez, "Push to Lower the Voting Age Gains Traction Across the States," NBC News, June 24, 2018.

Chapter 10: Real Representation

179

"I don't remember meeting the governor": Sarah Lyall and Richard Fausset, "Stacey Abrams, a Daughter of the South, Asks Georgia to Change," *New York Times,* October 26, 2018.

She vowed to one day return: Terrell Jermaine Starr, "Stacey Abrams' Political Rise Is Georgia's Coming-to-Jesus Moment," The Root, November 6, 2018.

"Black folk have lived on these lands": Yashwant Raj, "Democrat Stacey Abrams Makes History, Becomes First Black Woman Nominated for Governor by a Major Party," *Hindustan Times,* May 23, 2018.

180

Across local, state, and federal offices: Alexa Lardieri, "Despite Diverse Demographics, Most Politicians Are Still White Men," *U.S. News,* October 24, 2017.

Women hold fewer than a quarter: Center for American Women and Politics, "2018 Election Night Tally," November 28, 2018.

Twenty states have never: Lauren Holter, "9 Women Were Elected Governor in the 2018 Elections—Matching the Previous Record," Bustle, November 7, 2018.

Only one state legislature in history: Olivia Exstrum, "Nevada Just Became the First State in History with a Majority-Female Legislature," *Mother Jones,* December 18, 2018.

181

Forty-seven out of fifty: Rutgers, "Fun Facts About American Governors," January 2018.

At the state level, people of color hold only 14 percent of legislative seats: New American Leaders Project, "States of Inclusion," 2016.

Latinx and Asian Americans: Antonio Flores, "How the U.S. Hispanic Population Is Changing," Pew Research Center, September 18, 2017.

But together they hold: Jamilah King, "The First Dreamer to Run for Office in New York Has a Message for Donald Trump," *Mother Jones,* September 12, 2018.

In 2018, roughly five hundred LGBTQ: Liam Stack and Catie Edmondson, "A 'Rainbow Wave'? 2018 Has More L.G.B.T. Candidates than Ever," *New York Times,* August 4, 2018.

Younger people are more likely: Samantha Allen, "Just How Many LGBT Americans Are There?," Daily Beast, January 14, 2017.

"Having LGBTQ people sitting": Liam Stack and Catie Edmondson, "A 'Rainbow Wave'? 2018 Has More L.G.B.T. Candidates than Ever," *New York Times,* August 4, 2018.

182

The consulting firm McKinsey: Thomas Barta, Markus Kleiner, and Tilo Neumann, "Is There a Payoff from Top-Team Diversity?," McKinsey & Company, April 2012.

A study published in Scientific American: Richard B. Freeman and Wei Huang, "Collaboration: Strength in Diversity," *Nature,* September 16, 2014.

"Diverse juries deliberated longer": Tufts University, "Racial Diversity Improves Group Decision Making in Unexpected Ways, According To Tufts University Research," *ScienceDaily,* April 10, 2006.

184

In reviewing recent research: Katherine W. Phillips, "How Diversity Makes Us Smarter," *Scientific American,* October 1, 2014.

"Often when people speak": Annie Ma, "William Tong Wants to Be Connecticut's First Asian American Attorney General, and He's 'Not Afraid' of Donald Trump," *Mother Jones,* September 7, 2018.

185

"The people closest to the pain": P.R. Lockhart, "In 2018, Black Women Like Ayanna Pressley Are Fighting for Political Power—and Winning," Vox, September 5, 2018.

They live longer, too: Susan Chira, "There's No Nice Lady Caucus in Congress," *New York Times,* November 10, 2018.

It's no surprise that a study: Sarah Anzia and Christopher Berry, "The Jackie (and Jill) Robinson Effect: Why Do Congresswomen Outperform Congressmen?," *American Journal of Political Science* 55, no. 3 (2011).

"The message that I heard loudly": Matthew Rozsa, "History Made This Week in Pennsylvania: 'It's Time for More Women in Government, Period,'" Salon, May 17, 2018.

186

Women in Congress are particularly: Susan Chira, "There's No Nice Lady Caucus in Congress," *New York Times,* November 10, 2018.

On average, compared to men: Susan Chira, "There's No Nice Lady Caucus in Congress," *New York Times,* November 10, 2018.

Bills they sponsor pass: Susan Chira, "There's No Nice Lady Caucus in Congress," *New York Times,* November 10, 2018.

They also bring, on average: Sarah Anzia and Christopher Berry, "The Jackie (and Jill) Robinson Effect: Why Do Congresswomen Outperform Congressmen?," *American Journal of Political Science* 55, no. 3 (2011).

And a recent study of 125 countries: Chandan Kumar Jha and Supipta Sarangi, "Women and Corruption: What Positions Must They Hold to Make a Difference?," *Journal of Economic Behavior & Organization* 151 (2018): 219–33.

When Eric Gonzalez Juenke of Michigan State University: Eric Gonzalez Juenke and Andy Henion, "Minority Political Candidates Just Need a Chance," Michigan State University, February 11, 2014.

Once minority candidates entered races: Para Shah, "To Understand Elective Officeholding by Minorities, Look at Who Runs for Election, Not Just Who Wins," The Society Pages, October 24, 2014.

187

Regardless of gender: Heather Caygle, "Poll: Partisan Gap Could Limit Women's Gains in November," *Politico Magazine,* June 5, 2018.

Roughly two out of every hundred Americans: Seth Motel, "Who Runs for Office? A Profile of the 2%," Pew Research Center, September 3, 2018.

Looking at all elections: Reflective Democracy Campaign, "Who Runs (in) America."

Male college students: Claire Cain Miller, "The Problem for Women Is Not Winning. It's Deciding to Run," *New York Times,* October 25, 2016.

188

College men were twice as likely: Claire Cain Miller, "The Problem for Women Is Not Winning. It's Deciding to Run," *New York Times,* October 25, 2016.

"It took 10 years volunteering": Claire Cain Miller, "The Problem for Women Is Not Winning. It's Deciding to Run," *New York Times,* October 25, 2016.

"To ensure that more women can serve and lead effectively": Cynthia Richie Terrell, "A Title IX for Women in Politics," *American Prospect,* August 30, 2016.

When Tammy Duckworth: Annika Neklason, "Moms Running for Office Are Finally Advertising Their Motherhood," *Atlantic Monthly,* July 23, 2018.

"Adjustments such as these": Colleen Shalby, "A Record Number of Women Are Running for Office. This Election Cycle, They Didn't Wait for an Invite," *Los Angeles Times,* October 10, 2018.

But Lawless and Fox's: Ezra Klein, "Beyond Hillary: By Invitation Only," *American Prospect,* June 20, 2008.

189

"Potential candidates who receive": Ezra Klein, "Beyond Hillary: By Invitation Only," *American Prospect,* June 20, 2008.

For instance, one study showed: New American Leaders Project, "States of Inclusion," 2016.

And in a study of state office holders: New American Leaders Project, "States of Inclusion," 2016.

Only 62 percent of Americans are white: Reflective Democracy Campaign, "Who Runs (in) America."

"It's the height of hypocrisy": Elaine Godfrey, "Why Aren't Top Democrats Acknowledging the Black Women Running for Office?," *Atlantic Monthly,* June 14, 2018.

190

"It's safe to say there are institutional barriers": Aaron Blake, "Yes, Politics Is Still Dominated by Old, White Men. Here's Why," *Washington Post,* September 3, 2014.

"Politics is not the kind of open": Alexa Lardieri, "Despite Diverse Demographics, Most Politicians Are Still White Men," *U.S. News,* October 24, 2017.

"For so long, African-Americans": Margaret Talbot, "The Women Running in the Midterms During the Trump Era: This Year's Wave of Female Candidates Has Some Striking Features Besides Its Sheer Size," *New Yorker,* April 18, 2018.

191

Nearly one hundred countries perform better: World Economic Forum, "The Global Gender Gap Report 2017," November 2, 2017.

Fifty-six out of 146 nations: Abigail Geiger and Lauren Kent, "Number of Women Leaders Around the World Has Grown, but They're Still a Small Group," Pew Research Center, March 8, 2017.

European countries that specifically work toward a target: Steven Hill, "Why Does the US Still Have So Few Women in Office?," *The Nation,* March 7, 2014.

Efforts have included the creation of a specific number of seats: Louise Davidson-Schmich, "How Does the US Compare with Other Countries in Terms of Women's Representation?," Vox, April 10, 2017.

In Spain, for example: Louise Davidson-Schmich, "How Does the US Compare with Other Countries in Terms of Women's Representation?," Vox, April 10, 2017.

192

For example, black women: Andre M. Perry, "Analysis of Black Women's Electoral Strength in an Era of Fractured Politics," Brookings Institution, September 10, 2018.

If black women do stick their necks out and run: Andre M. Perry, "Analysis of Black Women's Electoral Strength in an Era of Fractured Politics," Brookings Institution, September 10, 2018.

"When it comes to women of color": Maya Salam, "A Record 117 Women Won Office, Reshaping America's Leadership," *New York Times,* November 7, 2018.

193

Historically, incumbents at all levels: Margaret Talbot, "The Women Running in the Midterms During the Trump Era: This Year's Wave of Female Candidates Has Some Striking Features Besides Its Sheer Size," *New Yorker,* April 18, 2018.

U.S. House incumbents have raised four times: Open Secrets, "Incumbent Advantage."

"It's not a talent gap": Alexa Lardieri, "Despite Diverse Demographics, Most Politicians Are Still White Men," *U.S. News,* October 24, 2017.

194

"A lot of the strategy is similar": Russell Berman, "How to Win Elections in a System 'Not Set Up for Us,'" *Atlantic Monthly,* July 30, 2018.

During Stacey Abrams' run for Georgia: Terrell Jermaine Starr, "Stacey Abrams' Political Rise Is Georgia's Coming-to-Jesus Moment," The Root, November 6, 2018.

195

"As a female prosecutor": Becca Andrews, Kanyakrit Vongkiatkajorn, and P.R. Lockhart, "13 Women Are Fighting to Get into the Senate. Here They Are in Their Own Words," *Mother Jones,* November 4, 2016.

Don't mention her young children: Name It. Change It., "Media Guide to Gender Neutral Coverage of Women Candidates and Politicians."

197

More than half of elections nationwide: Seth Motel, "Who Runs for Office? A Profile of the 2%," Pew Research Center, September 3, 2018.

They urge parties to ask: New American Leaders Project, "States of Inclusion," 2016.

198

"When the U.S. helped Afghanistan": Becca Andrews, Kanyakrit Vongkiatkajorn, and P.R. Lockhart, "13 Women Are Fighting to Get into the Senate. Here They Are in Their Own Words," *Mother Jones,* November 4, 2016.

She intends to run again: Megan Keller, "Stacey Abrams Says She May Run for Senate or Governor in Coming Years," *The Hill,* December 4, 2018.

"We will all, at some point, encounter": Caroline Clarke, "18 Uplifting, Ass-Kicking Stacey Abrams Quotes," *Black Enterprise,* August 27, 2018.

203

"I'm not naive": Dale Russakoff, "Lessons of Might and Right," *Washington Post,* September 9, 2001.

"It was kind of shocking": Anna North, "America's Sexist Obsession with What Women Politicians Wear, Explained," Vox, December 3, 2018.

"In my family, there were no girl chores": Maya Salam, "A Record 117 Women Won Office, Reshaping America's Leadership," *New York Times,* November 7, 2018.

"It is so important to remember": Kevin Liptak, "Michelle Obama Hits Back Against 'Hateful' Rhetoric," CNN, April 6, 2016.

Chapter 11: Voter Turnoff

205

"It made me feel like voting": Clint Hendler, "I Know I'm Dying and This Will Be My Last Vote," *Mother Jones,* November 6, 2018.

In 2014, 144 million Americans: David Becker, "A New Approach to Reversing the Downward Spiral of Low Turnout," *Stanford Social Innovation Review,* February 11, 2016.

In the 2016 presidential election: 270 to Win, "2016 Presidential Election."

If "did not vote": Alex Ward, "Why US Voter Turnout Lags Behind Other Advanced Democracies," Vox, November 6, 2018, and Editorial Board, "Vote. That's Just What They Don't Want You to Do," *New York Times,* March 10, 2018.

In 2018, less than half: Emily Stewart, "Early Numbers Suggest Voter Turnout Soared in the 2018 Midterms," Vox, November 7, 2018.

206

With so little participation: David Becker, "A New Approach to Reversing the Downward Spiral of Low Turnout," *Stanford Social Innovation Review,* February 11, 2016.

207

Black and white women: Alicia Parlapiano and Adam Pearce, "For Every 10 U.S. Adults, Six Vote and Four Don't. What Separates Them?," *New York Times,* September 14, 2016, and United States Elections Project, "Voter Turnout Demographics."

The superrich, the top 1 percent: Sean McElwee, "Why the Voting Gap Matters," Demos, October 23, 2014.

Turnout for older people: Kelly Born, "Increasing Voter Turnout: What, If Anything, Can Be Done?," *Stanford Social Innovation Review, April 26, 2016,* and Circle, "Five Takeaways on Social Media and the Youth Vote in 2018," November 15, 2018.

208

The winner (Yancey) was determined: John Bacon, "And the Winner Is . . . Republican Wins After Name Drawn from a Bowl in Virginia House Race," *USA Today,* January 4, 2018.

That same year, Colorado had seven: Colorado Election Results, "Coordinated Election," November 7, 2017.

Class is the best predictor of whether or not someone votes: Jan Leighley and Jonathan Nagler, *Who Votes Now? Demographics, Issues, Inequality, and Turnout in the United States* (Princeton University Press, 2013).

Turnout tends to be lowest among hourly workers: Adam Bonica and Michael McFaul, "Want Americans to Vote? Give Them Election Day Off," *Washington Post,* October 11, 2018.

"Both nonvoters and voters support": Sean McElwee, "Why Voting Matters," Demos, September 16, 2015.

209

Likewise, Leighley found: Asma Khalid, Don Gonyea, and Leila Fadel, "On the Sidelines of Democracy: Exploring Why So Many Americans Don't Vote," NPR, September 10, 2018.

Interestingly, nonvoters: Benjamin Wallace-Wells, "Sanders, Trump, and the Rise of the Non-Voters," *New Yorker,* April 1, 2016.

And the second-highest turnout: Lori Robertson, "Sanders' Shaky Turnout Claim," Factcheck.org, June 6, 2016.

Nonvoters' leanings: Lori Robertson, "Sanders' Shaky Turnout Claim," Factcheck.org, June 6, 2016.

210

Almost three-quarters of Americans surveyed: Drew Desilver, "U.S. Trails Most Developed Countries in Voter Turnout," Pew Research Center, May 21, 2018.

Almost all (91 percent) say voting: Pew Research Center, "The Public, the Political System and American Democracy," April 26, 2018.

Pew found that 43 percent: "Why Are Millions of Citizens Not Registered to Vote?," The Pew Trusts, June 21, 2017.

211

"I tried to register for the 2016 election": Rachel Bashein, Zak Cheney-Rice, Amelia Schonbek, and Emma Whitford, "12 Young People on Why They Probably Won't Vote," *New York,* October 30, 2018.

Megan, age twenty-nine: Jamelle Bouie, "Why Don't Young People Vote? This System Doesn't Want Them To," Slate, November 5, 2018.

"Typically, I check way before that time": Rachel Bashein, Zak Cheney-Rice, Amelia Schonbek, and Emma Whitford, "12 Young People on Why They Probably Won't Vote," *New York,* October 30, 2018.

Of people who are registered: Wendy R. Weiser, "Automatic Voter Registration Boosts Political Participation," *Stanford Social Innovation Review,* January 28, 2016.

212

The requirement to register to vote: Sean McElwee, "Why Voting Matters," Demos, September 16, 2015.

Turnout in the United States is lower: Alicia Parlapiano and Adam Pearce, "For Every 10 U.S. Adults, Six Vote and Four Don't. What Separates Them?," *New York Times,* September 14, 2016.

The Pew Research Center ranked the United States: Drew Desilver, "U.S. Trails Most Developed Countries in Voter Turnout," Pew Research Center, March 21, 2018.

Turnout tends to be highest in countries: Drew Desilver, "U.S. Trails Most Developed Countries in Voter Turnout," Pew Research Center, March 21, 2018.

Universal registration: Evan Halper, "Hillary Clinton Attacks Republicans over Voting Restrictions," *Los Angeles Times,* June 4, 2015.

214

Even though twenty-three-year-old Reese: Rachel Bashein, Zak Cheney-Rice, Amelia Schonbek, and Emma Whitford, "12 Young People on Why They Probably Won't Vote," *New York,* October 30, 2018.

They reported confusion about the voting process: Campus Vote Project, "Best Practices to Help Students Register and Vote: A Guide for Colleges and Universities."

"Everyone is promoting registering": Rachel Bashein, Zak Cheney-Rice, Amelia Schonbek, and Emma Whitford, "12 Young People on Why They Probably Won't Vote," *New York,* October 30, 2018.

A study out of Tufts University found: Asma Khalid, Don Gonyea, and Leila Fadel, "On the Sidelines of Democracy: Exploring Why So Many Americans Don't Vote," NPR, September 10, 2018.

And the Pew Research Center found that six: "Who Votes, Who Doesn't, and Why," Pew Research Center, October 18, 2006.

"It is very hard to get voters' attention": Tina Rosenberg, "Increasing Voter Turnout for 2018 and Beyond," *New York Times,* June 13, 2017.

216

While seventeen states and Washington, D.C.: Brennan Center for Justice at New York University School of Law, "Automatic Voter Registration," November 7, 2018.

They require people to fill out separate forms: Stuart Naifeh, "Accelerating the Vote: How States Are Improving Motor-Voter Registration Under the National Voter Registration Act," Demos, July 7, 2017.

If all states reach even 75 percent: Sean McElwee, "Why Voting Matters," Demos, September 16, 2015.

"A key flaw in the U.S. elections system": Sean McElwee, "Why Voting Matters," Demos, September 16, 2015.

217

In just a year, more than a quarter of a million: Jamelle Bouie, "Why Don't Young People Vote? This System Doesn't Want Them To," Slate, November 5, 2018.

More than one hundred thousand: Niraj Chokshi, "Automatic Voter Registration a 'Success' in Oregon," *New York Times,* December 2, 2016.

"Studies of voter registration systems": Wendy R. Weiser, "Automatic Voter Registration Boosts Political Participation," *Stanford Social Innovation Review,* January 28, 2016.

"Automatic Voter Registration will make voting more accurate": U.S. Pirg, "With Unanimous Bipartisan Vote, Automatic Voter Registration Bill Passes Massachusetts Senate."

218

Nonprofit VOTE found that citizens: Kevin Robillard, "Which State Had Top Turnout?," *Politico Magazine,* March 12, 2013.

219

In 2016, Cynthia Perez of Phoenix, Arizona: Fernanda Santos, "Angry Arizona Voters Demand: Why Such Long Lines at Polling Sites?," *New York Times,* March 24, 2016.

Both had long waits: Jim Malewitz, "In Some Counties, Early Voting Means Long Lines," *Texas Tribune,* October 24, 2016.

"I got my ballot in the mail": David Roberts, "Voting by Mail Is Fair, Safe, and Easy. Why Don't More States Use It?," Vox, May 27, 2017.

Three—Colorado, Oregon, and Washington: National Conference of State Legislatures, "All-Mail Elections (aka Vote-By-Mail)," August 8, 2018.

220

"Each additional communication": Elizabeth Bergman, "Voting Only by Mail Can Decrease Turnout. Or Increase It. Wait, What?," *Washington Post,* December 21, 2015.

221

"Election integrity is ensured": Phil Keisling and Sam Reed, "Voting at Home Will Help Save Our Democracy," *New York Times,* September 19, 2018.

In her survey of people who'd previously voted: Elizabeth Bergman, "Voting Only by Mail Can Decrease Turnout. Or Increase It. Wait, What?," *Washington Post,* December 21, 2015.

"It felt deliberative": David Roberts, "Voting by Mail Is Fair, Safe, and Easy. Why Don't More States Use It?," Vox, May 27, 2017.

"A wide swath of research shows": Wendy R. Weiser, "Automatic Voter Registration Boosts Political Participation," *Stanford Social Innovation Review,* January 28, 2016.

For instance, Anthony Fowler: Peter Dreier, "Democrats Must Mobilize America's Largest Political Party: Nonvoters," *American Prospect,* November 23, 2016.

222

They found some practices: John D. Sutter, "Hawaii: The State That Doesn't Vote," CNN, October 24, 2012.

Highlight what is at stake: Nonprofit Vote, "Seven Tips on Getting Out the Vote," 2012.

Those who can visualize themselves voting: Nonprofit Vote, "Seven Tips on Getting Out the Vote," 2012, and Campus Election Project, "Build Momentum," 2018.

People respond better to friends: Nonprofit Vote, "Seven Tips on Getting Out the Vote," 2012.

"Maybe the most effective is a close friend": "Why people don't vote, and what to do about it," *Science News,* November 4, 2016.

Finally, time your efforts to the final weeks: Nonprofit Vote, "Seven Tips on Getting Out the Vote," 2012.

Election Day reminders: Donald P. Green, "The Effects of an Election Day Voter Mobilization Campaign Targeting Young Voters," Circle, September 2004.

If you persuade one new voter: Nonprofit Vote, "Seven Tips on Getting Out the Vote," 2012.

"Thirty to 50 percent of people": Kelly Born, "Increasing Voter Turnout: What, If Anything, Can Be Done?," *Stanford Social Innovation Review,* April 12, 2016.

223

Women in Switzerland were given the vote: Luca Powell, "What Democracy and Voting Rights Look Like Around the World," Global Citizen, November 8, 2016.

Even today, women in Afghanistan, Pakistan, Uganda: Georgia Aspinall, "Here Are the Countries Where It's Still Really Difficult for Women to Vote," *Grazia,* June 2, 2018.

Elections in Saudi Arabia are rare: Luca Powell, "What Democracy and Voting Rights Look Like Around the World," Global Citizen, November 8, 2016.

And there are no elections: Who Rules Where, "Most People in the World Can't Vote"—a Refutation," April 20, 2015.

The battle for the right to vote: Amanda Uren, "1908–1917 Imprisoned Suffragettes," Mashable.

224

Young people are 40 percent: Yvote, "We Have a Crisis in Youth Voter Turnout in the United States."

Simply showing high school students: Civic Youth, "Young Voter Mobilization Tactics."

225

"Four million people turn 18 this year": Daniel Ducassi, "Parkland Teens Launch Nationwide Bus Tour to Boost Voter Turnout Among Young People," *Politico Magazine,* June 4, 2018.

229

"Change is hard": Elizabeth Warren's Facebook Page, April 14, 2016.

"We do not have a government": Allan J. Lightman, *The Embattled Vote in America* (Cambridge, Mass.: Harvard University Press, 2018).

"If we are to maintain the principle": Calvin Coolidge, "Address Before the Daughters of the American Revolution," Washington, D.C., April 19, 1926, Calvin Coolidge Presidential Foundation.

The biggest hurdle: David Weigel, "Alexandria Ocasio-Cortez: The Democrat who challenged her party's establishment—and won," *Denver Post,* June 27, 2018.

Chapter 12: Let's Fix Our Democracy!

232

Voters in more than half of the states: Brennan Center for Justice at New York University School of Law, "Congressional Redistricting Guide."

235

Mari Copeny, who began advocating: Nicole Gallucci, "Little Miss Flint's 5 Awesome Tips for Becoming a Young Activist," Mashable, September 22, 2018.

236

"We will be unable to address the big challenges": Jeff Merkley, "Merkley Unveils Sweeping Blueprint to Restore American Democracy," January 2, 2019.

237

They control state elections, too: Constitution Center, "Legislative Branch."

In 2018, measures to reduce the influence of money: Elena Nunez and Jay Riestenberg, "Democracy on the Ballot," Common Cause, October 24, 2018.

238

One study showed that state legislatures: Glen Justice, "States Six Times More Productive than Congress," Connectivity, January 27, 2015.

239

The report found that "social change in the U.S.": Alex Tribou and Keith Collins, "This Is How Fast America Changes Its Mind," Bloomberg, June 26, 2015.

"Though the pattern": Alex Tribou and Keith Collins, "This Is How Fast America Changes Its Mind," Bloomberg, June 26, 2015.

240

"We are the only ones who haven't used this valuable tool": Citizens Take Action, "The Solution."

"Each state has its own constitution": Ezra Klein, "The Rigging of American Politics," Vox, October 16, 2018.

241

"Better policy decisions": Congressional Management Foundation, "Citizen-Centric Advocacy: The Untapped Power of Constituent Engagement."

242

Almost a quarter give phone calls: Seth Turner, "CMF Trains Citizen Advocates on What to Do Before, During, and After Meetings," Congressional Management Foundation, March 7, 2018.

"If you want democracy to work effectively": Kathy Goldschmidt, "Why You Shouldn't Contact Senators and Representatives Who Don't Represent You," Congressional Management Foundation, April 17, 2017.

"It's really a missed opportunity": Tanzina Vega, "Vote, but Your Civic Engagement Doesn't End There," WNYC Studios, January 21, 2019.

243

Letters to the editor: Congressional Management Foundation, "Citizen-Centric Advocacy: The Untapped Power of Constituent Engagement."

"Our research has shown": CMF, "More Research Demonstrates the Ineffectiveness of Mass Email Campaigns to Congress," Congressional Management Foundation, January 9, 2019.

A stunning 94 percent surveyed: Congressional Management Foundation, "Citizen-Centric Advocacy: The Untapped Power of Constituent Engagement."

Ninety-nine percent said: Congressional Management Foundation, "Citizen-Centric Advocacy: The Untapped Power of Constituent Engagement."

"In-person meetings are the easiest way": Congressional Management Foundation, "Citizen-Centric Advocacy: The Untapped Power of Constituent Engagement."

"Each time the process is easy": Congressional Management Foundation, "Citizen-Centric Advocacy: The Untapped Power of Constituent Engagement."

248

In the meeting be sure to cover: Seth Turner, "CMF Trains Citizen Advocates on What to Do Before, During, and After Meetings," Congressional Management Foundation, March 7, 2018.

Most lawmakers (85 percent according to the CMF): Congressional Management Foundation, "Citizen-Centric Advocacy: The Untapped Power of Constituent Engagement."

"When a Member of Congress meets a constituent": Bradford Fitch, "Fitch: What Really Motivates Members of Congress?," *Roll Call,* February 27, 2012.

249

"Congress wins [when] it gets information": Seth Turner and Chip Felkel, "Citizen Engagement: What Works and What Doesn't," Congressional Management Foundation, August 15, 2018.

"I was very nervous for this trip": Wendy Heath, "My First Lobbying Experience: A Report from D.C.," Clean Water Action, May 3, 2016.

250

Roughly 20 percent: Tanzina Vega, "Vote, But Your Civic Engagement Doesn't End There," WNYC Studios, January 21, 2019.

"Together our results show": A. Madestam, D. Shoag, S. Veuger, and D. Yanagizawa-Drott, "Do Political Protests Matter? Evidence from the Tea Party Movement," *Quarterly Journal of Economics,* December 4, 2011.

251

Ninety-five percent of legislators surveyed: CMF, "Members of Congress Work 70 Hours a Week—But Think It's Worth It," Congressional Management Foundation, March 12, 2013.

Nearly half of registered voters reported: Congressional Management Foundation, "Citizen-Centric Advocacy: The Untapped Power of Constituent Engagement."

One U.S. Senate office saw a 900 percent: Tanzina Vega, "Vote, but Your Civic Engagement Doesn't End There," WNYC Studios, January 21, 2019.

252

"The hardest part was just starting": Smart Girls staff, "Following the 2016 Election, Katie Fahey—then 26-Years-Old—Decided She Wanted to Bring People Together to Solve One of Our Democracy's Most Pressing Issues," Amy Poehler's Smart Girls, October 29, 2018.

"If we start to show we're paying attention": Veronica, "Madison Kimrey Fights For Young Voters!," Sweety High, May 7, 2014.

"For every person who speaks up": Veronica, "Madison Kimrey Fights for Young Voters!," Sweety High, May 7, 2014.

"My story could be the story of anyone": Veronica, "Madison Kimrey Fights for Young Voters!," Sweety High, May 7, 2014.